When Innovation Moves at Digital Speed

The Digital Future of Management

Paul Michelman, series editor

How to Go Digital: Practical Wisdom to Help Drive Your Organization's Digital Transformation

What the Digital Future Holds: 20 Groundbreaking Essays on How Technology Is Reshaping the Practice of Management

When Innovation Moves at Digital Speed: Strategies and Tactics to Provoke, Sustain, and Defend Innovation in Today's Unsettled Markets

When Innovation Moves at Digital Speed

Strategies and Tactics to Provoke, Sustain, and Defend Innovation in Today's Unsettled Markets

MIT Sloan Management Review

The MIT Press
Cambridge, Massachusetts
London, England

This book was set in Stone and Neue Haas Grotesk by the MIT Press. Printed and bound in the United States of America.

Library of Congress Cataloging-in-Publication Data

Names: Sloan Management Review Association.
Title: When innovation moves at digital speed : strategies and tactics to provoke, sustain, and defend innovation in today's unsettled markets / MIT Sloan Management Review.
Description: Cambridge, MA : MIT Press, [2018] | Series: The digital future of management | Includes bibliographical references and index.
Identifiers: LCCN 2017061373 | ISBN 9780262535717 (pbk. : alk. paper)
Subjects: LCSH: Organizational change. | Business enterprises--Technological innovations. | New products--Management.
Classification: LCC HD58.8 .W4764 2018 | DDC 658.4/063--dc23 LC record available at https://lccn.loc.gov/2017061373

10   9   8   7   6   5   4   3   2   1

Contents

Series Foreword

Books in the Digital Future of Management series draw from the print and web pages of *MIT Sloan Management Review* to deliver expert insights and sharply tuned advice on navigating the unprecedented challenges of the digital world. These books are essential reading for executives from the world's leading source of ideas on how technology is transforming the practice of management.

Paul Michelman
Editor in Chief
MIT Sloan Management Review

Introduction: Innovation at Digital Speed

Scott D. Anthony

I have spent close to two decades helping leaders at large organizations confront the challenges of disruptive change. In the early days, my clients either came from the handful of industries characterized by rapid change or were run by a vanguard of forward-thinking executives. That has changed.

Consider, for example, the late-afternoon phone call that came to Innosight LLC's Singapore office in August 2016. The call was from Siam Cement Public Co. Ltd. The organization, which goes by the name SCG, is an institution in Bangkok, Thailand, with a commanding presence in cement and other building materials, basic chemicals, and packaging. SCG was founded more than 100 years ago at the decree of King Vajiravudh (Rama VI), and today employs more than 50,000 people and reports annual revenues of more than $10 billion. Its question: How might we accelerate digital transformation? When a company that produces cement, cardboard boxes, and commodity chemicals in an emerging market asks that question, it becomes clear that digitalization has led to innovation becoming *the* issue of our time.

Leaders in almost every organization are thinking about what digital means for their business and, specifically, how digital forces will drive their approaches to innovation. Indeed, more than 70% of respondents to a recent Innosight survey reported making significant investments in some form of digital innovation. Almost 80% of respondents expect to increase their investments in digital transformation over the next five years. Leaders are making these investments with optimism—almost 50% of respondents said they consider digital technologies to primarily present opportunities versus 25% who primarily view digitalization as a threat; the remainder view it as a mix of both.

That said, one of our general observations is that few organizations have clearly defined their *digital ambition*. Ideally, that ambition should map out the scale (how much), speed (at what pace), and scope of investment in digital technology. For most organizations, defining scope is the most challenging. Scope is where you will play in digital transformation. How will you shift current strategy for the digital realm? What new opportunities will you pursue? What new opportunities *won't* you pursue? In determining the scope of their digital ambitions, leaders need to take into account the three dimensions of digitalization.

The first area to consider is *digitizing current operations*. Using digital technologies to optimize core operations is increasingly a competitive necessity. Every organization should determine ways to drive efficiency, enhance performance, and increase agility. For example, Sime Darby Berhad, a leading conglomerate in Kuala Lumpur, Malaysia, is building the "plantation of the future" in its palm oil business unit (which it plans to spin out into a separate organization in 2018). Advanced genomics will boost yields by up to 15%. Ubiquitous sensors, artificial intelligence, and drone-based monitoring connected via a proprietary platform will help to monitor and optimize the nutrient and moisture level of each tree, optimizing plantation utilization. Autonomous vehicles, robotics, and exoskeletons on plantation workers will further boost productivity. As data pours into a centralized control room, a manager can oversee multiple plantations remotely. The net result will be greater land utilization, higher productivity, and improved performance on key sustainability metrics.

The next area to explore is *digitizing the customer interface.* One of the first commercial uses of the internet was for retailers and banks to create websites (and then mobile sites) to communicate and transact directly with customers. Airlines followed suit via digital check-in machines. Today, fast-food companies are introducing touchscreen kiosks that facilitate order customization and streamline kitchen operations. Continued advancements in underlying technologies provide additional ways for companies to further digitize the interface with customers, allowing them to better serve more customers. These changes aren't just for consumer-facing companies, however. For example, SCG customers can buy its building materials on the web and via Line, a popular messaging app in Thailand. SCG has also implemented chatbots to further support e-commerce sales of building materials.

Digitizing operations and the customer interface enables companies to capture richer data about operations, customer preference, and more. Augmenting this kind of information with data generated by sensors and user activity on devices like tablets, smartphones, and interactive televisions provides insights for improving existing offerings and inventing new ones. Thus, the final area to consider is *creating new digital business models.*

Digitalization creates opportunities for companies to create powerful new growth businesses. One option is to become a digital *producer* that provides actionable insights based on rich data. Consider how The Weather Co. LLC (owned by IBM) blends historical and real-time meteorological data produced by a large variety of sensors to develop unique predictive insights. Its data scientists then work with retailers and consumer brands to adjust merchandising and promotions based on weather predictions. The second option is to become a digital *platform*. Much has been written about powerful platforms that have emerged in the transport (Uber, Grab, Didi) and hotel (Airbnb) industries. Incumbents are getting into the game. For instance, General Electric Co. is undertaking a well-publicized effort to turn Predix into the platform for the "industrial internet." By 2016, GE Digital's revenues crossed $7 billion. That's still a tiny fraction of the conglomerate's global revenues, but it took digital powerhouse Netflix 19 years to cross a similar threshold.

The pages that follow teem with practical advice for advancing efforts across the three dimensions of digitalization. Further, they reinforce several common themes that recur in the broader innovation literature.

The first theme is that *magic happens at intersections*, where different mindsets and skills collide. Leaders seeking to accelerate digital innovation should find ways to maximize connections inside and outside their organization. A decade after Procter & Gamble Co. showed the power of open innovation, organizations are finding creative ways to bring more voices into the innovation process. In "Collaborating with Customer Communities: Lessons from the Lego Group," Yun Mi Antorini, Albert M. Muñiz Jr., and Tormod Askildsen provide a fascinating overview of how the Lego Group has engaged the more than 100,000 active adult fans in its communities. More and more companies realize they need to do a better job of driving internal intersections. Michael Arena, Rob Cross, Jonathan Sims, and Mary Uhl-Bien share cogent guidance in "How to Catalyze Innovation in Your Organization," showing how "brokers," "connectors," and "energizers" can enable "adaptive spaces" inside organizations to help them thrive. Finally, the opening article in Part IV, "When Innovation Meets the Language of the Corner Office," demonstrates how—gasp!—consultants can learn from innovators, and vice versa.

The second important theme emphasizes *the value of action over analysis*. Every innovative idea is partially right and partially wrong. The trick in the early stage of innovation is knowing it is impossible to tell which part is which. Most organizations confront this challenge by seeking truth through analysis. That is, they run focus groups, talk to experts, and build elaborate financial forecasts, all in the hopes of building a perfect plan. There is no such thing. The only way to develop a winning plan is through trial-and-error experimentation.

Want to maximize the impact of intersectional magic? Read "Developing Innovative Solutions through Internal Crowdsourcing," in which Arvind Malhotra, Ann Majchrzak, Lâle Kesebi, and Sean Looram provide practical guidance for running internal crowdsourcing campaigns. Want to create industry-changing—indeed, even world-changing—innovation? Reflect on the lessons of Joseph V. Sinfield (who was a member of Innosight's leadership team for a dozen years) and Freddy Solis's fascinating description of how "lily pad" strategies accelerate category-creating innovations in "Finding a Lower-Risk Path to High-Impact Innovations."

The next reinforcing theme is how *innovation success requires thinking beyond technology*. Too many people still think that innovation is the sole purview of the white lab coat–wearing scientist toiling away in an isolated corner of the organization. But innovation isn't the job of the few—it is the job of the many. And even the most pathbreaking technology will struggle unless supported by the right development and commercialization approach. That point is made painfully clear in Duncan Simester's contribution, "Why Great New Products Fail." In "Developing New Products in Emerging Markets," Srivardhini K. Jha, Ishwardutt Parulkar, Rishikesha T. Krishnan, and Charles Dhanaraj describe how Cisco Systems Inc. built a successful research and development lab in India in part by forming an innovative partnership with a local engineering services company to help bootstrap early innovation efforts. And in "Learning the Art of Business Improvisation," Edivandro Carlos Conforto, Eric Rebentisch, and Daniel Amaral show how innovating the innovation process itself can improve the odds of creating successful products and services.

Finally, *When Innovation Moves at Digital Speed* explores how *the greatest enemy lies within.* Organizations are built to do what they are currently doing with ever-improving precision. Innovation involves doing something different. Therefore, innovators often encounter fierce internal resistance. For example, no one doubts that design thinking principles accelerate innovation success. But if companies don't deal with the sociological challenges detailed in "Why Design Thinking in Business Needs a Rethink," they will struggle to realize the full value of investment in building these important capabilities. It's a well-established fact that business model innovation can drive innovation success, but change often meets internal resistance. Innosight cofounder Clayton M. Christensen and his coauthors describe in "The Hard Truth about Business Model Innovation" how incumbents can be hostile homes for would-be innovators of business models. "Managing Tensions between New and Existing

Business Models" further explains how to anticipate and manage the friction that inevitably comes with doing new things. And "Creating Better Innovation Measurement Practices" shows how power struggles can sometimes poison the pursuit of useful innovation metrics.

Driven by the forces of digitalization, the last two decades have seen a true transformation in how the world views innovation. Historically, most have perceived innovation to be a mystical, magical act practiced by a select few with rare genetic gifts. We now know that innovation is a discipline that can be measured, managed, and improved with careful practice. No doubt that many challenges remain. But repeatable success draws closer.

Make no mistake: innovation is hard work. Yet, it is hard to be in the innovation field and not be an optimist at heart. The practical guidance in *When Innovation Moves at Digital Speed* will help to turn optimism into innovation success.

I

Tactics to Boost Innovation

1

How to Catalyze Innovation in Your Organization

Michael Arena, Rob Cross, Jonathan Sims, and Mary Uhl-Bien

Economists have estimated that approximately 50% of annual growth in US GDP can be attributed to product and service innovation, and more than 90% of executives claim that long-term organizational success depends on developing and implementing new ideas.[1,2]

Research shows that growth fueled through organic innovation is more profitable than growth driven by acquisition, in part because the organizational capability required is vastly different.[3,4] Yet organic, or *emergent*, innovation typically does not occur without heroic effort in many large organizations. While technology giants such as Alphabet, Apple, and Facebook are lionized for their innovative cultures, other industries struggle with hierarchal organizations that make consistent organic innovation very difficult.

Companies try to address this by formalizing innovation processes. However, such programs, when they succeed, often produce only a portion of the growth that most large organizations require.[5] Many innovation programs fail to meet expectations, in part because they separate the innovation process from the informal networks needed to adapt and support an innovation.[6]

For example, "skunk works" programs have some lauded successes but also many failures because their innovations have been developed outside the social ecosystem of the organization. Similarly, acquisition strategies that attempt to bring in new expertise and creative ideas make logical sense but far too often underperform due to integration challenges.[7] Of course, these stories of failure often don't make it to press, so those less effective approaches persist.

Leaders need to better support emergent innovation to supplement planned new product or service development activities. Our research suggests that, rather than leaving emergent innovation to serendipity, executives should create collaborative contexts where innovation is likely to emerge from unpredictable pockets of creativity. Importantly, managers need to stimulate these kinds of environments in a thoughtful way that does not simply overload employees with new collaborative demands from formal matrix structures, multiple "part-time" team assignments, or collaborative technologies that overtax people and that too often kill creativity and innovation.[8]

Emergent innovation occurs when entrepreneurial individuals within an organization incubate and advance new ideas for addressing customer needs and dynamically changing market conditions.[9] *How do we best connect employees in ways that more systematically unleash emergent innovation?* This is the question we set out to explore in a decade-long partnership between researchers and organizational leaders.

About the Research

Our research, conducted over a decade, focused on tracing commercially successful (and unsuccessful) innovations back to their origins. While successful innovations spanned the organization and had many originators, unsuccessful ideas were typically isolated to one part of the organization, and we were almost always able to find the originator in the first or second interview.

The first phase of this work focused on conducting over 400 interviews on successful and unsuccessful innovations as well as employing organizational network analysis to analyze the network dynamics of scores of institutions.

The second phase of work entailed interviewing 160 high-performing leaders (80 men and 80 women) across 20 well-known organizations in financial services, software, consumer products, retail, professional services, manufacturing, and life sciences. These interviews captured rich stories of how leaders had successfully introduced an innovation and, importantly, how they had managed both the innovation and the network to achieve success.

While the first stage of our work showed the importance of networks in identifying who leaders should engage in different kinds of innovation efforts, the second phase provided the blueprint for how successful innovators brought an idea to fruition by simultaneously developing the innovation and working with the network.

Part of the answer lies in the power of network structures and the ability of organizations to create what we have termed *adaptive space*.[10] We define adaptive space as the network and organizational context that allows people, ideas, information, and resources to flow across the organization and spur successful emergent innovation. Adaptive space facilitates the movement of innovative ideas and information across a system. It works by enabling ideas generated in entrepreneurial pockets of an organization to flow into the operational system and develop into new products or services that lead to growth.

Adaptive space is not a physical building or lab such as an incubator or accelerator (although both offer great potential for sharing, creating, and developing ideas). Instead, adaptive space within organizations is fluid and can shift based on need.

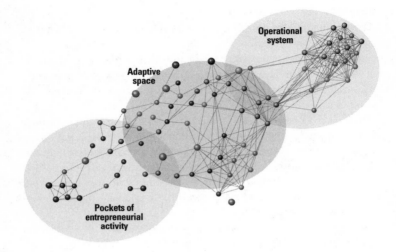

The Role of Adaptive Space

Adaptive space is the network and organizational context that allows people, ideas, information, and resources to flow across the organization and spur successful emergent innovation. It is not a physical space but instead is any environment—such as a hackathon or internal crowd-sourcing event—that creates an opportunity for ideas generated in entrepreneurial pockets of an organization to flow into its operational system.

Companies create adaptive space through environments that open up information flows and enrich idea discovery, development, and amplification. That can be done in a number of ways. For example, Noblis, a nonprofit research corporation headquartered in Reston, Virginia, created adaptive space through an internal crowdsourcing initiative, while General Motors Co. has generated adaptive space through events that bring together people from different parts of the organization.

Creating Adaptive Space through Crowdsourcing

Noblis is a nonprofit research corporation that consults to governments on science and technology issues such as data analytics, cybersecurity, and networking. Historically, Noblis relied on independent science and research programs to explore new ideas and develop new capabilities. To make this work, a few well-connected principal investigators would submit proposals to top management for endorsement. However, as Noblis grew, its leadership recognized that the organization had to become more collaborative to remain competitive. "We have smart people everywhere," said CEO and President Amr ElSawy, "but we don't always know what their interests are."

In 2015, the leadership team changed the discovery process. Using a crowdsourcing platform, employees generated ideas for innovative research and client-driven projects. The firm created methods to solicit ideas, not fully developed proposals, from employees. Two senior leaders reached out to colleagues across all areas of expertise to solicit comments on any idea, leading to fine tuning and energy naturally gathering around some projects more than others. Since individuals were asked to submit ideas of interest, they became more energized to engage in the process of sharing.

The first year, the process generated hundreds of project ideas and all received numerous comments; more than half of employees gave feedback. From the initial suggestions, about 100 ideas were selected for further development and full proposals. Of those, more than two dozen research projects were approved and given resources.

The new approach led to several powerful innovation, network, and talent outcomes, including:

- **A shift in culture from more adversarial (idea generator versus senior leader, or project versus project) to collaborative:** The crowdsourcing approach began to build a culture of conversation, which carried over to ongoing project reviews and funding meetings.

- **More expansive idea generation and development:** By replacing the top-down and "inner-circle" approach to the research agenda with a range of divergent perspectives early on, the company has been able to harness the collective intelligence of the organization more effectively—and profitably.

- **Increased employee engagement and alignment from transparency:** People voluntarily "killed" their projects and supported others. Decisions were made that supported the whole rather than protected turf.

- **A wider recognition of talent across the business:** Many ideas and insights were brought forth by employees who were below the radar or working in remote offices. Two-thirds of the funded projects were led by newcomers to the process.

Using network analysis and data collected from more than 400 interviews, we found that innovation leaders within an organization engaged with experts, influencers, and decision makers through different phases of an innovation's journey, and in the process managed to substantially expand the impact of their innovation and streamline its acceptance as it moved from concept to implementation.

We address this topic by exploring employee networks and the social nature of innovation, how to identify and manage the three network roles critical for emergent innovation—brokers, connectors, and energizers—and how individuals can drive emergent innovation in adaptive space.

Adaptive Space at General Motors

At General Motors Co., GM 2020, an initiative launched in 2014, creates adaptive space to spark the movement of ideas and information across the organization. The result has been many emergent innovations. For example, one group created a new process to improve buyer–supplier relationships, another developed a millennial-friendly interviewing process, and yet another created monthly cross-departmental sessions designed to share problems and proactively identify organizational roadblocks.

A GM 2020 event could take the form of a Co-Lab, a Summit, a Tipping Forward event or any number of employee-developed constructs. A Co-Lab, for example, is a 24-hour intensive challenge. As many as 60 individuals from across different groups within the company compete in small teams and pitch ideas to executives. A Co-Lab operates on the premise that sometimes the best solutions emerge when you have the least time. Challenges include everything from customer service opportunities to product design ideas to employee engagement issues. Challenges center on the user and employ design thinking principles to bring customers into the process.

A Summit includes as many as 300 individuals acting as brokers and connectors from across functions, using design thinking methods to share, create, and build solutions. A Tipping Forward event, which typically involves 100 to 200 individuals, provides the adaptive space necessary to openly share the many successes that have already been applied locally, and then tap into the passion of energizers to amplify these successes across the broader enterprise.

GM 2020 also encourages individuals to leverage their networks to create their own solutions. For example, a small group of engineers and researchers launched an internal "maker space" to encourage cross-group tinkering. An internal learning community held an event to unleash more creativity across functions. Another group launched internal "TEC Talks" (technology, engineering, and creativity), featuring monthly presentations from internal experts.

The Social Nature of Innovation

Tales of a lone inventor with a blinding insight are unhelpful myths when it comes to corporate innovation.[11] Successful service, product, or process innovations within large, complex organizations are very much a social phenomenon. This is why organizations that are routinely innovative are intentional about enabling individuals to engage and connect in ways that trigger and expand ideas.[12] They know it is imperative to leverage organizational networks to allow innovation to emerge and be incorporated into the organization's formal operational system.[13]

Recent advances in computing power, coupled with the proliferation of collaborative technologies, have made assessing these networks easier than ever before. Consider a portion of a network diagram of information flow within a roughly 10,000-person research and development (R&D) unit of a consumer products organization.

In this diagram, the dots reflect scientists, the lines reflect who is turning to whom for information, and the two colors reflect two different scientific disciplines that should have been working closely together. The diagram shows clearly that large-scale collaboration between the two groups was not occurring the way leaders expected at this juncture. This lack of collaboration was also occurring at 42 other points in the overall network; mapping the relationships allowed us to see this.

The organization found that working through key network roles was essential to success. Many good ideas never come to fruition because people do not have the formal or informal influence to get them into play. In the consumer products organization, leaders had sponsored ideation sessions with key experts selected from the two technical domains, believing that

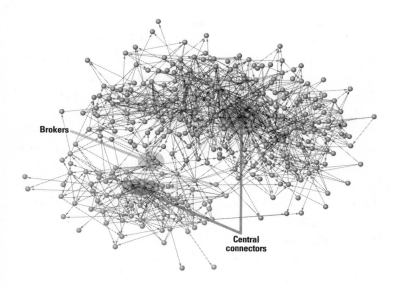

Key Roles in a Network

This diagram represents information flows in a portion of the network within a research and development (R&D) unit of a consumer products organization. The orange and green colors reflect two different scientific disciplines that should have been working more closely together—but the network diagram reveals that large-scale collaboration wasn't occurring between the groups. People who are well connected within their subgroup are central connectors, while those whose connections span groups are brokers. In large organizations, brokers often introduce ideas and central connectors develop them.

interesting innovations would emerge from bringing smart people together in a creative dialogue. What happened was quite different. Without the network analysis information in hand, the leaders selected people based on reputation. These leaders always ended up engaging the well-connected people *within* each area—those commonly thought of as "essential." (These people are what we call *central connectors*.) The "essential" individuals were also often the ones most wedded to their scientific paradigms and, sometimes, to their reputations. As a result, they were less effective at visualizing possibilities across groups. It was only when the leaders began to include lower-level employees with connections between the silos that the organization began to get integrative ideas and see emergent innovation flourish. (We call such bridge-building individuals *brokers*.)

Network mapping provides a valuable tool in that it enables much more targeted innovation efforts. But these efforts can take hold only if adaptive space exists to cultivate both the innovation *and* the network that generates it. Because large, bureaucratic organizations are designed for efficiency through division of labor, their traditional structures limit the potential for innovation. Adaptive space is needed to connect these divided channels and allow ideas to advance from the entrepreneurial (informal) to the operational (formal) system. Such adaptive space allows for networked interactions to foster the creation of ideas, innovation, and learning.

Three Network Roles

A key to catalyzing emergent innovation is identifying and positioning innovators within an organization. Doing so requires an understanding of individual roles within organizational networks. The social capital necessary for evoking emergent innovation is best represented by three roles: brokers, central connectors, and energizers.

What Brokers, Central Connectors, and Energizers Do.

Brokers, central connectors, and energizers all play important roles in successful innovation processes within large organizations. While brokers and central connectors represent distinct positions in a network, energizers can be anywhere in a network; they can be brokers, central connectors, or other individuals.

Brokers	Central Connectors	Energizers
Connect different groups in networks	Are well connected in a subgroup	Can be anywhere in a network
Bridge silos	Get things done	Provide support
Explore and seek new ideas	Organize others	Inspire others to act
Have diverse perspectives	Serve as experts	Fully engage in the moment
Focus on many things	Quickly solve problems	Strive toward vision

Brokers

As mentioned earlier, brokers build bridges from one group to another within and outside an organization. As a result, they act as critical conduits of information and ideas. Specifically, brokers offer three competitive advantages to an organization: broader access to diverse information, early access to new information, and control over the diffusion of the information. New insights usually arise at the intersection of existing networks. That is, as two heterogeneous groups connect, the potential for novelty increases. Brokers facilitate this discovery process through their social connections and then determine how and when these insights can be introduced to other parts of the organization. The creation of adaptive space enables brokers to more actively connect and navigate beyond their local subgroups to explore new possibilities. For example, in one pharmaceutical company, the innovation process could be traced to a few key scientists who were brokers to outside academics. When two of these brokers left the organization, critical relationships were lost; the result was a significant decline in the innovation rate for the company.

Examples of adaptive space and brokering are often studied between organizations (rather than within). One well-known example is Procter & Gamble Co.'s Connect + Develop program, which relies on external sources of innovation coupled with internal screening to allow P&G executives to identify new customer needs or possible product extensions, and then execute. The Connect + Develop program works on the premise that in an increasingly connected world, inspiration and innovation are the result of deliberate brokering relationships between the organization and external partners that generate value creation. Connect + Develop has led to novel products such as the Mr. Clean Magic Eraser.[14]

Central Connectors

While brokers are outstanding at finding ideas, they are not always best positioned to drive implementation. This is where group cohesion and central connectors play a critical role. Group cohesion represents how connected individuals are to one another within a group. A group is considered cohesive when many redundant connections exist among group members. That is, the likelihood of any individual within the group being connected to any other individual within the group is high. As a result, cohesive groups can quickly share information and generally operate with high levels of trust.[15]

Connectors, especially those relatively central to cohesive groups, are essential to the development and implementation process. They are well positioned to garner support for ideas from within a given group. Once introduced by a central connector, these ideas are easily diffused across the more tightly connected subgroup.[16] Furthermore, the level of trust within these subgroups facilitates engagement with the ideas, learning, and risk taking—all crucial components of creativity and development.[17] As a result, connectors can quickly drive local applications of ideas as well as future iterations for improvement.

The "dailies" at Pixar Animation Studios in Emeryville, California, illustrate the kind of trust cohesive subgroups can have. Every day, creators at the company present the projects they are working on to get critical feedback. In most organizations, individuals finish their work before submitting it for critique. However, at Pixar, individuals trust that their colleagues have their best interest in mind, and thus the in-progress reviews enable more creativity. The teams at Pixar believe dailies are a critical contributor to producing high-quality, innovative films.[18]

Innovation in a social context requires a thorough understanding of the interplay between brokers and connectors. This is why adaptive space is so critical: It helps position individuals within the network to drive progress. Consider the history of Hewlett-Packard Co., whose name was once synonymous with innovation. In its glory days, HP created a work environment that encouraged flexibility and innovation. At HP, the policy was to move engineers between major projects over time. The result was the movement of key learnings and technologies to

new projects, where they could be reconfigured into new combinations and applications. As a former HP senior engineer once
described it, "I had to work in a single field for only two or three
years and then, like magic, it was a whole new field—a para-
dise for creativity."[19] HP executives intuitively knew that if they
moved people around, knowledge would flow more readily. In
essence, HP provided the space that enabled an active interplay
between brokers and connectors.

In large organizations, brokers often introduce ideas and central connectors develop them.[20] Central connectors are often
limited to insulated subgroups and therefore are likely to have
their ideas dismissed by the larger organization.[21] Furthermore,
cohesive groups are good at developing incremental innovations
but rarely promote disruptive concepts.[22] Individuals within a
cohesive group are less likely to take a major risk that could jeop-
ardize their local group status. While the level of trust within
these groups promotes risk taking (and thus some forms of innovation), social acceptance limits the extent of these risks. The
result: more, but safer, bets.

Energizers

Energizers help push people beyond the safe bets. In an organizational network, energizers may be brokers, central connectors,
or simply other individuals who enthusiastically adopt an idea
and promote it. Energizers trigger the interest and engagement
of others and unleash the passion necessary for bold innovations
to advance. Network energy, or enthusiasm, drives diffusion,
cocreation, and active engagement across the larger organization. It challenges people to think more boldly than they would
within their own subgroups and creates a contagious mindset as
the innovation progresses.

Energizers are able to fully engage in interactions, inspiring others to devote more time and energy to an initiative.[23] The reputation of an energizer spreads quickly across the network, attracting others to aggregate multiple ideas into bolder, integrated concepts that are more likely to succeed.[24] Energizers connect with individuals who have different expertise or backgrounds. These differences can be embraced as elements essential to the creation of bolder innovation. The result is the potential for new, more robust possibilities to emerge.

W.L. Gore & Associates Inc., a materials science company based in Newark, Delaware, embraces such possibilities by giving employees freedom to both dabble with new ideas and act as energizers who share these ideas throughout the broader network. Then, a cross-functional review called "Real, Win, Worth" scrutinizes the concepts.[25] The intent of these peer reviews is to bring together people from varying backgrounds to challenge the fitness of a concept and ensure that it can win in the marketplace and make money for the company. In response to the scrutiny, the associate is challenged to experiment and learn with low-risk solutions. The result for W.L. Gore has been a multitude of innovative products and solutions that have been stretched beyond their original concepts.

Lessons for Innovators

So far, we have focused on the leadership implications of managing networks to drive emergent innovation. But our research also yielded important insights for individuals, by revealing *how* individuals' collaborative activities play a critical role in all phases of a successful innovation. For example, every successful innovation we studied involved a noninsular network early in the problem-solving stage that helped the individual reframe the problem space and generate a more substantive solution and impact. Similarly, each success also benefited from ideas that other people brought and/or serendipitous encounters that dramatically shaped the course of the innovation. Overall, what was perhaps most striking to us in this work was the degree to which innovation had to occur in both the product or service and the network for success to unfold. The network was important not only in the generation of the idea but also in acceptance of the innovation. Successful innovators were innovating on both levels—the innovation and the network—following five principles, outlined below.

Tap into adjacent expertise and a broad network early in problem solving. Almost universally, more successful innovators did not immediately solve a problem they were given. Whether asked by their board, boss, client, or a demanding coworker to address a significant problem, they were likely to ask questions and engage their network early to help them think about the problem differently and to find people with tangentially relevant expertise who might give them a different perspective on the solution. In contrast, less successful people were more likely to jump into the work without engaging adjacent expertise to reconceptualize the problem space. Interestingly, a good number of this latter group did solve problems and generate solutions. However, relative to the more successful people, this group solved smaller problems or produced less innovative outcomes over time. This group fell behind the other group and never really knew why. Even at this nascent stage, there is an interplay between the network, the nature of the innovation, and its likely success.

Our quantitative models and interview subjects found boundary-spanning ties as critical to innovation success over time. Consider four types of ties:

- **Emergence or creativity ties:** Identify silos or boundaries where value could be created by bridging two thought worlds—typically across expertise domains, functions, clients, and cultures.

- **Capability development ties:** Connect with people whom you normally seek out or who voluntarily offer you feedback—whether on work, interaction, or decision-making topics.

- **Depth or best practice transfer ties:** Identify others with similar expertise—across geography, company, or functional lines—where connections could help promote depth, currency, or efficiency in your work.

- **Sense-making or political awareness ties:** Seek out people or practices that help you get an accurate picture of the network and how to position ideas.

Make early interactions beneficial to others. The more successful innovators we studied sought to draw others to their ideas, rather than push their needs and seek help by mandate. Establishing mutual benefit was much more likely to create vibrant exchanges, vest other people in the outcome, and lead to successful innovation. This mattered in a significant but surprising way: Every successful innovation benefited at some point in the trajectory of the solution by a surprise insight, resource, or idea coming to the seeker. Invariably, these fortuitous developments had a material impact on the success of the project, but the seeker would never have been able to predict or foresee this. In contrast, less successful people were more likely to jump directly into their project without either establishing a personal connection to others or making a concerted effort to be helpful to them. As a result, they were far less likely to benefit from surprises from an extended network.

The lesson is this: Go into every interaction with a clear goal so that you are respectful of others' time. But engage in a way that benefits the other person and thus draws him or her into the relationship. Build people's trust by connecting personally, asking questions and shaping what you know to their needs, giving recognition and status, looking for ways you can benefit the people you have sought out, and creating positive energy in your interactions with them.

Spread ownership of the idea and seek feedback. Hub-and-spoke models of innovation—where individuals put themselves at the center of the network of interactions and coordinate all efforts and ideas—were rare and worked only in transactional settings. In fact, among our interviewees, trying to develop an idea in isolation until it was seen as bulletproof was a sure recipe for failure. The more successful innovators made decisions on whom to include and how to run initial meetings in ways that shaped both the innovation and the network. To be sure, they were quick to get the right expertise into the room and use open, divergent brainstorming processes to mold the innovation. But they were equally likely to diffuse ownership early, invite naysayers, and test ideas externally with key opinion leaders to help seed the network's acceptance of the innovation. Rather than shield an idea until it was perfected, they created conditions that engaged others in developing the idea.

The lesson? As you begin to form a nexus around an innovation, use facilitation techniques that create openness early. Focus on the *why* of the work to help engender a sense of purpose and commitment, and require teammates to reach out to source ideas with clients, stakeholders, experts, and network opinion leaders. Engage key opinion leaders and naysayers early. They bring needed information and insight to the project and later, as ambassadors, provide legitimacy and boost adoption. Innovation is more successful when ideation and development are diffused and contributors have pride of ownership. Great collaborative outcomes are generated when people share values and understand why the work is important.

Develop a prototype early. Be open in process but insist on pushing to a prototype as early as possible. Throughout our interviews, prototypes were essential and took a wide range of forms. They could be working code, small-scale models, or full solutions. Early prototypes provide proof of concept. But even more important is that a working prototype dramatically changes the nature of the conversation and engagement with the network. With a prototype established, the exchanges become more targeted in terms of enhancements needed. More subtly, a prototype establishes trust that something can be accomplished and thus moves the innovation and network forward to a solution. As one leader suggested, "If we have a proof of concept or pilot, that is the right time to engage the negative people. A model speaks louder and does not require them to just trust me."

You will know you are on the right track when others are telling your story. Proactively engaging others builds "benevolence-based trust" (trust that you have others' interests in mind), while showcasing the prototype builds "competence-based trust" (trust that you can do what you say).[26]

Communicate the early-stage solution and then iterate within the network. In moving from prototype to solution rollout, two core activities matter. First, have a broad, inclusive, and collaborative communication process. Look for rich stories that engage people on an emotional level. For example, one leader made the case for change: "The story was not to make people afraid but to show we have a massive opportunity. Framing the narrative in terms of possibility instead of threat was key. After a few meetings of vision and opportunity, they bought in. Success for me was when a couple [of] important stakeholders started telling the story for me. They made it their own."

Second, it is critical to create forums and secure time and resources to adapt the innovation based on feedback. The biggest surprise for most leaders we interviewed was how much work they had to do at this stage, and the amount of adaptation needed when they thought their work was largely done. As more stakeholders and end users give input, ensure that your team is prepared to make incremental changes, test, and adapt quickly. As one leader indicated, "We needed to evolve significantly from our early thinking—75 percent of the functionality changed based on those stakeholder meetings."

The Adaptive Space Imperative

For a large organization, innovation is both essential and increasingly difficult. Innovating requires managers to grapple with a conundrum: How does one empower those with innovative ideas (in entrepreneurial pockets within the organization), while ensuring that their best ideas are effectively implemented (using the organizational operational system)?

The value of networks and adaptive space is that they enable influential people to tell stories about an innovation they are championing in ways that echo across the network. As these stories spread, others are attracted to engage, and the network of those engaged begins to include critical stakeholders, therefore enhancing the likelihood of organizational support for the innovation. Our research suggests that by understanding social networks and developing an adaptive space, even seemingly bureaucratic organizations can facilitate emergent innovations.

Notes

1. US Chamber of Commerce Foundation, "Enterprising States 2015: States Innovate" (Washington, DC: US Chamber of Commerce, 2015).

2. D. Smith and C. Mindrum, "How to Capture the Essence of Innovation," *Accenture Outlook Journal* 1 (January 2008): 1–10.

3. T. Davila, M. Epstein, and R. Shelton, *Making Innovation Work: How to Manage It, Measure It, and Profit from It* (Upper Saddle River, NJ: FT Press, 2012).

4. A. G. Lafley and R. Charan, *The Game-Changer: How You Can Drive Revenue and Profit Growth with Innovation* (New York: Crown Business, 2008).

5. J. Hagedoorn and N. Wang, "Is There Complementarity or Substitutability Between Internal and External R&D Strategies?" *Research Policy* 41, no. 6 (2012): 1072–1083; and A. Kandybin, "Which Innovation Efforts Will Pay?" *MIT Sloan Management Review* 51, no. 1 (2009): 53.

6. R. Cross, P. Gray, S. Cunningham, M. Showers, and R. J. Thomas, "The Collaborative Organization: How to Make Employee Networks Really Work," *MIT Sloan Management Review* 52, no. 1 (2010): 83–90; M. E. Johnson-Cramer, S. Parise, and R. Cross, "Managing Change through Networks and Values," *California Management Review* 49, no. 3 (2007): 85–109; and R. Cross, C. Ernst, D. Assimakopoulos, and D. Ranta, "Investing in Boundary-Spanning Collaboration to Drive Efficiency and Innovation," *Organizational Dynamics* 44, no. 3 (2015): 204–216.

7. M. M. Bekier, A. J. Bogardus, and T. Oldham, "Why Mergers Fail," *McKinsey Quarterly* (Autumn 2001): 6–9; M. E. Graebner, K. M. Eisenhardt, and P. T. Roundy, "Success and Failure in Technology Acquisitions: Lessons for Buyers and Sellers," *Academy of Management Perspectives* 24, no. 3 (2010): 73–92; and D. R. King, D. R. Dalton, C. M. Daily, and J. G. Covin, "Meta-Analyses of Post-Acquisition Performance: Indications of Unidentified Moderators," *Strategic Management Journal* 25, no. 2 (2004): 187–200.

8. R. Cross, R. Rebele, and A. Grant, "Collaborative Overload," *Harvard Business Review* 94, no. 1–2 (2016): 74–79; and R. Cross and P. Gray, "Where Has the Time Gone?" *California Management Review* 56, no. 1 (2013): 50–66.

9. G. Oster, "Characteristics of Emergent Innovation," *Journal of Management Development* 29, no. 6 (2010): 565–574.

10. M. Uhl-Bien and M. Arena, "Complexity Leadership: Enabling People and Organizations for Adaptability," *Organizational Dynamics* 46, no. 1 (2017): 9–20.

11. A. Hargadon, *How Breakthroughs Happen: The Surprising Truth About How Companies Innovate* (Boston: Harvard Business Press, 2003); A. Hargadon and R. I. Sutton, "Technology Brokering and Innovation in a Product Development Firm," *Administrative Science Quarterly* 42, no. 4 (1997): 716–749; and J. Singh and L. Fleming, "Lone Inventors as Sources of Breakthroughs: Myth or Reality?" *Management Science* 56, no. 1 (2010): 41–56.

12. M. de Jong, N. Marston, and E. Roth, "The Eight Essentials of Innovation," *McKinsey Quarterly*, April 2015, https://www.mckinsey.com/business-functions/strategy-and-corporate-finance/our-insights/the-eight-essentials-of-innovation.

13. Uhl-Bien and Arena, "Complexity Leadership"; and M. Uhl-Bien and R. Marion, "Complexity Leadership in Bureaucratic Forms of Organizing: A Meso Model," *Leadership Quarterly* 20, no. 4 (2009): 631–650.

14. L. Huston and N. Sakkab, "Connect and Develop: Inside Procter & Gamble's New Model for Innovation," *Harvard Business Review* 84, no. 3 (2006): 58–66.

15. L. Fleming, S. Mingo, and D. Chen, "Collaborative Brokerage, Generative Creativity, and Creative Success," *Administrative Science Quarterly* 52, no. 3 (2007): 443–475.

16. R. Reagans and B. McEvily, "Network Structure and Knowledge Transfer: The Effects of Cohesion and Range," *Administrative Science Quarterly* 48, no. 2 (2003): 240–267.

17. T. M. Amabile, S. G. Barsade, J. S. Mueller, and B. M. Staw, "Affect and Creativity at Work," *Administrative Science Quarterly* 50, no. 3 (2005): 367–403.

18. E. Catmull, "How Pixar Fosters Collaborative Creativity," *Harvard Business Review* 86, no. 9 (2008): 63–72.

19. L. Fleming, "Finding the Organizational Sources of Technological Breakthroughs: The Story of Hewlett-Packard's Thermal Ink-Jet," *Industrial and Corporate Change* 11, no. 5 (2002): 1059–1084.

20. R. Cross, W. Baker, and A. Parker, "What Creates Energy in Organizations?" *MIT Sloan Management Review* 44, no. 4 (2003): 51–57.

21. R. S. Burt, "Structural Holes and Good Ideas," *American Journal of Sociology* 110, no. 2 (2004): 349–399.

22. J. Battilana and T. Casciaro, "Overcoming Resistance to Organizational Change: Strong Ties and Affective Cooptation," *Management Science* 59, no. 4 (2013): 819–836.

23. R. Cross, J. Linder, and A. Parker, "Charged Up: Managing the Energy That Drives Innovation," *Management Quarterly* 48, no. 2 (2007): 14–29.

24. Cross, Baker, and Parker, "What Creates Energy in Organizations?"

25. J. Rao, "W. L. Gore: Culture of Innovation," case no. BAB698 (Babson Park, MA: Babson College, 2012).

26. D. Z. Levin and R. Cross, "The Strength of Weak Ties You Can Trust: The Mediating Role of Trust in Effective Knowledge Transfer," *Management Science* 50, no. 11 (2004): 1477–1490.

2

Harnessing the Secret Structure of Innovation

Martin Reeves, Thomas Fink, Ramiro Palma, and Johann Harnoss

In an era of low growth, companies need innovation more than ever. Leaders can draw on a large body of theory and precedent in pursuit of innovation, ranging from advice on choosing the right spaces to optimizing the product development process to establishing a culture of creativity.[1] In practice, though, innovation remains more of an art than a science.

But it doesn't need to be.

In our research, we made an exciting discovery.[2] Innovation, much like marketing and human resources, can be made less reliant on artful intuition by using information in new ways. But this requires a change in perspective: We need to view innovation not as the product of luck or extraordinary vision but as the result of a deliberate search process. This process exploits the underlying structure of successful innovation to identify key information signals, which in turn can be harnessed to construct an advantaged innovation strategy.

Comparing Innovation Strategies

Let's illustrate the idea using Lego bricks. Think back to your childhood days. You're in a room with two of your friends, playing with a big box of Legos (say, the beloved "fire station" set). All three of you have the same goal in mind: building as many new toys as possible. As you play, each of you searches through the box and chooses the bricks you believe will help you reach this goal.

Let's now suppose each of you approaches this differently. Your friend Joey uses what we call an impatient strategy, carefully picking Lego men and their firefighting hats to immediately produce viable toys. You follow your intuition, picking random bricks that look intriguing. Meanwhile, your friend Jill chooses pieces such as axles, wheels, and small base plates that she noticed are common in more complex toys, even though she is not able to use them immediately to produce simpler toys. We call Jill's approach a patient strategy.

At the end of the afternoon, who will have developed the most new products? That is, who will have built the most new toys? Our simulations show that this depends on several factors. In the beginning, Joey will lead the way, surging ahead with his impatient strategy. But as the game progresses, fate will appear to shift. Jill's early moves will begin to seem serendipitous when she's able to assemble complex fire trucks from her choice of initially useless axles and wheels. It will appear that she was lucky, but we will soon see that she effectively harnessed serendipity.

What about you? Picking components randomly, you will have built the fewest toys. Your friends had an information-enabled strategy, while you relied only on intuition and chance.

What can we learn from this? If innovation is a search process, then your component choices today matter greatly in terms of the options they will open up to you tomorrow. Do you pick components that quickly form simple products and give you a return *now*, or do you choose the components that give you a higher *future* option value?

In our research, we analyzed the mathematics of innovation as a search process for viable product designs across a universe of components. We then tested our insights using historical data on innovations in four real environments. We ran simulations based on detailed data from four domains: software technologies, culinary arts, music, and language. In the process, we made a surprising discovery. You can have an advantaged innovation strategy by using information about the unfolding process of innovation. But there isn't one superior strategy. The optimal strategy is both time dependent and space dependent—there are many innovation spaces, each of which has its own characteristics. In innovation, as in business strategy, winning strategies depend on context.

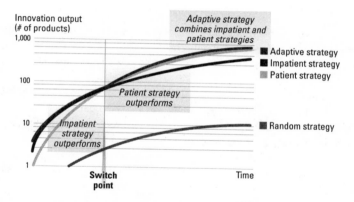

Information-Enabled Innovation Strategies Perform Better

Our analysis indicates that strategies that take into account information about the unfolding innovation process tend to outperform random innovation strategies that don't use such information. We also found that, in the early phase of the development of an innovation space, an *impatient* strategy outperforms; in later stages, a *patient* strategy does. Finally, it is possible to have an *adaptive* strategy—one that switches from impatient to patient as an innovation space develops and that outperforms in all phases of the space's development.

Source: BCG Henderson Institute and London Institute

Our research demonstrates three crucial insights.

First, information-enabled strategies outperform strategies that do not use the information generated by the search process. Second, in an earlier phase of the development of the innovation space, an impatient strategy outperforms; in later stages, a patient strategy does. Critically, third, it is possible to have an *adaptive* strategy, one that changes as a market develops and that outperforms in all phases of the market's development. Developing an adaptive strategy requires you, in effect, to know when to switch from Joey's approach to Jill's. The switching point is knowable and occurs when the complexity of products starts to level off after increasing.

About the Research

We analyzed innovation as a process of combining components to make new products. We used simulations based on historical data to study this process in four domains: software technologies, gastronomy, language, and music.[3]

In software, the products we studied were software programs and the components were development tools. We collected data for 1,200 software products made up of 1,000 development tools from StackShare, a website that catalogs tools used by technology companies.

In gastronomy, the products we examined were recipes and the components were ingredients. We collected data for 58,000 recipes made from 381 ingredients from the recipe websites allrecipes.com, epicurious.com, and menupan.com.

In language, the products we studied were words and the components were letters. We used as our data the words in the official word list for Scrabble tournaments and the 26 letters in the English alphabet.

In music, the products we studied were jazz bands of the early 20th century and the components were musicians. We collected data for 1,000 bands made up of 4,700 musicians from the Red Hot Jazz archive, a website that catalogs pre-1930 jazz bands.

Applying the Insight

From our findings, we distilled a five-step process for constructing an information-advantaged innovation strategy.

Step 1. Choose Your Space: Where to Play?

The features of your innovation space matter, so it's important to make a deliberate choice about where you want to compete. Interestingly, it's not enough to analyze markets or anticipate customers' needs. To innovate successfully, you also need to understand the structure of your innovation space.

Start by taking a snapshot of key competing products and their components. How complex are the products, and do you have access to the components? As a rule of thumb, choose spaces where product complexity is still low and where you have access to the most prevalent components. By focusing on immature spaces, you can get ahead of competitors by first employing a rapid-yield, impatient strategy and then later switching to a more patient strategy with delayed rewards. Uber Technologies Inc. provides a good example. The company entered the embryonic peer-to-peer ride-sharing space three years after it was founded in 2009 as a limousine commissioning company. Uber chose its space wisely: The ride-sharing industry was immature, product complexity was low, and the necessary components were easily accessible. The impatient strategy was to get to market quickly with a ride-sharing app. There is also now what appears to be a patient strategy at work at Uber—self-driving technology with a much higher level of complexity and a much longer gestation period.

Step 2. Select Your Strategy: How to Play?

Next, do something counterintuitive: Look backward, not forward. Measure the evolution of complexity in the innovation space you have chosen by analyzing the distribution of product sizes in terms of the number of unique components in products. If complexity is low and stable, it's an indication that the space is still in its infancy. Here, choose an impatient strategy. If complexity is high, then the space is maturing and a patient strategy will be the best approach. The complexity of a space is thus a crucial signal to orient your innovation strategy.

How can you extract this signal from the data in your space? Reassuringly, many innovators already have the tools to do so: Companies routinely reengineer competitors' products, analyze the patent landscape, and conduct interviews with technology experts to guide their operational decisions. We believe innovators can and should also use the same tools and information to guide their strategy by methodically measuring the evolution of product complexity in their space. This requires developing a taxonomy of components by sampling competitors' products and dissecting not only physical components but also intangible ones like process innovations or business model choices. While we are not aware of any company that is yet explicitly doing this, we do see that many startups implicitly follow this logic by shifting from an impatient minimum viable product logic to a more patient innovation strategy centered on more complex designs once cash flow and funding have been secured and the space begins to mature.

Step 3. Apply Your Strategy: How to Execute?

Next, execute your chosen innovation strategy. If you follow an impatient approach, your objective is to adopt or develop components that enable you to bring relatively simple products to market quickly. Ask yourself how you can be first, increasing your research and development (R&D) speed and decreasing time to market. A minimum viable product approach, which favors simplicity and speed, embodies such a strategy.

However, if the characteristics of your chosen innovation space imply that a patient strategy is more appropriate, a minimum viable product approach isn't the best; instead, your objective should be to maximize future innovation options. Large technology companies such as Apple Inc. and Samsung Group implicitly do this. They research and patent widely, but then often take years to integrate their innovations into new products—not because they are slow to innovate but precisely because they are playing a patient innovation game.

Can companies follow both a patient and an impatient approach in different parts of their business? They can—but it's a very hard thing to do well. General Electric Co., for example, has developed and widely implemented a program called FastWorks, which is essentially a capability to build and scale minimum viable products in rapid iteration cycles. However, GE also appears to be keeping its more traditional, patient innovation approach in place—in other words, it's ambidextrous with respect to innovation.[4] But few companies have GE's range of capabilities, so proceed with caution if pursuing such a strategy.

Step 4. Sense Shifts and Adapt: How to Extract a Switch Signal?

Next, let's remind ourselves that the best strategy is space and time dependent. This means you not only need to monitor the complexity of your innovation space but also must compete on access to information in order to detect valuable strategy-switching signals earlier than competitors. What acts as a switch signal? In our research, we found that a flattening in the increase of product complexity is a reliable signal that it is time to switch from an impatient innovation strategy to a patient one.

Licensing partnerships and technology acquisitions can be valuable to surface this signal. Most innovators use them to broaden their access to components in order to innovate faster. Equally important, however, is that such tactics can also provide innovators with broader information about the evolution of complexity in the space—and thus give them an information advantage in extracting a switch signal. A related tactic is the creation and orchestration of developer ecosystems (like those created by content managing platform Box Inc., open-source computing company Red Hat Inc., Apple Computer Inc., and others). These ecosystems are, in essence, managed innovation spaces where the orchestrator not only gains access to components and innovations developed by others but also has a unique gateway to extensive information on the space.

Step 5. Brace for Disruptions: How to Reset the Clock?

The promise of an information-enabled innovation strategy extends to disruption. Disruption, as seen through the lens of our model, is an event that suddenly resets and resimplifies an innovation space by lowering product complexity. We observe such events when two previously unconnected innovation spaces merge, giving rise to myriad new product innovations with reduced complexity. This implies that disruptions don't just happen—they are created by innovators at the edge of a space who build simpler products that leverage components from a different space. A classic example is the disruption of the music media industry by edge players in peer-to-peer file sharing (such

An innovator following this new information-enabled approach will — to its competitors and the public — appear to be minting its own luck.

as Napster, in its initial incarnation) and research organizations developing new music encoding standards (like the Munich, Germany–based research organization Fraunhofer-Gesellschaft, which was the main developer of MP3 technology for digital audio). While we cannot claim that we can predict such disruptions (yet), our analytical approach allows innovators to spot such events and interpret them as early warning signals.

A disruption always requires innovators to reset their innovation strategy and to return to an impatient approach. We modeled different responses to disruption in the technology space and found that companies that successfully reset their strategy have an innovation output that's about 50% higher than companies that don't.

Switching back to impatient behavior is easier said than done, because it requires a switch in all aspects of the innovation approach.

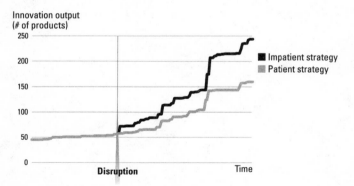

Navigating a Disruption
Our analysis suggests that the best response to a disruption is to switch from a patient to an impatient innovation strategy. Doing so successfully results in an innovation output that's roughly 50% higher than the output obtained by sticking with a patient strategy after a disruption.
Source: BCG Henderson Institute and London Institute

An Advantaged Innovation Strategy

Can you have an innovation strategy that is inherently advantaged? Our research suggests it is possible. In fact, an innovator following this new information-enabled approach will—to its competitors and the public—appear to be minting its own luck. Such an innovator will typically outperform others that do not use information in the same way.

Aspiring innovators seeking to adopt an information-enabled innovation strategy should take these five imperatives to heart:

- Reframe innovation as an information-enabled search process.
- Collect information on components and innovations to characterize the space.
- Analyze the maturity of the space, and adapt your strategy accordingly.
- Build an information advantage to innovate your approach to innovation itself.
- Respond to or create disruption by adapting your managerial approach.

Interestingly, this perspective on innovation has implications for other domains of problem solving. In a world where many simple problems have been solved, we are increasingly left with more complex ones for which impatient, linear problem-solving approaches offer little value. Our progress and prosperity will depend increasingly on solving hard problems that require less direct and more patient strategies. Whether addressing the challenges of innovation or issues of a broader societal nature, holding a patient line can be hard and risky. But a structured approach to problem solving as we describe in this chapter, guided by the right signals, will lead us more predictably to powerful solutions.

Notes

1. See, for example, W. C. Kim and R. Mauborgne, *Blue Ocean Strategy: How to Create Uncontested Market Space and Make the Competition Irrelevant*, expanded edition (Boston, MA: Harvard Business Review Press, 2015) on choosing spaces; B. Brown and S. Anthony, "How P&G Tripled Its Innovation Success Rate," *Harvard Business Review* 89, no. 6 (2011): 64–72, on product development; or L. de Brabandere and A. Iny, *Thinking in New Boxes: A New Paradigm for Business Creativity* (New York: Random House, 2013) on creativity in business.

2. See T. M. A. Fink, M. Reeves, R. Palma, and R. S. Farr, "Serendipity and Strategy in Rapid Innovation," March 2017, https://arxiv.org/abs/1608.01900.

3. Details of some of our analyses can be found in Fink et al., "Serendipity and Strategy in Rapid Innovation."

4. M. Little, "Innovation and What's Next," webcast presentation, September 15, 2014, http://www.ge.com.

3

Developing Innovative Solutions through Internal Crowdsourcing

Arvind Malhotra, Ann Majchrzak, Lâle Kesebi, and Sean Looram

As organizations look for better solutions to their everyday problems, many are encouraging their employees to use their experiences to develop new ideas and play a more active role in the innovation process. Whether the issue involves improving hiring practices, deciding which new products or services to offer, or creating better forecasts, companies including AT&T Inc., Google Inc., and Deutsche Telekom AG have turned to what's known as internal crowdsourcing.[1]

Although external crowdsourcing, which involves soliciting ideas from consumers, suppliers, and anyone else who wants to participate, has been widely studied, internal crowdsourcing, which seeks to channel the ideas and expertise of the company's own employees, is less well understood.[2] It allows employees to interact dynamically with coworkers in other locations, propose new ideas, and suggest new directions to management. Because many large companies have pockets of expertise and knowledge scattered across different locations, we have found that harnessing the cognitive diversity within organizations can open up rich new sources of innovation. Internal crowdsourcing is a particularly effective way for companies to engage younger employees and people working on the front lines.[3]

We conducted a four-year study of how multiple companies used internal crowds that included frontline employees to
find new solutions to business challenges. We observed internal crowdsourcing in practice, interviewed executives who
sponsored internal crowdsourcing innovation challenges, and
surveyed participants. We also participated in the design, implementation, and execution of internal crowdsourcing events at
several companies. In this article, we will examine the benefits
of internal crowdsourcing, the roadblocks that stand in the way
of successful initiatives, and ways crowdsourcing efforts can be
designed to overcome those roadblocks.

About the Research

This article is based on a four-year, multimethod research project with
companies engaged in internal crowdsourcing. In one part of our
research, we conducted in-depth analyses at three large organizations
(one in health care, one in telecommunications, and one in retail), and
we conducted interviews with the executives in charge of the internal
crowdsourcing. At the health care organization we studied, the chief
medical officer was in charge of engaging frontline employees in the
internal crowdsourcing process; two of us provided guidance and oversaw the execution of the company's internal crowdsourcing effort. At
the telecommunications company, we worked with a senior executive in
charge of the internal crowdsourcing effort. At fashion and retail company Li & Fung Ltd., we had access to the ideas, documents, and thinking process behind the design of an internal crowdsourcing event.

In addition, we collected data related to platforms and the design
of incentives for crowdsourcing challenges at seven other companies,
which were identified through a university-affiliated innovation center.
They included a distribution company, a Scandinavian telecommunications company, a US-based telecommunications infrastructure company, a data storage and analytics company, a graphics design software
company, an industrial products company, and an e-commerce platform
provider. Our partner at each organization was either the chief innovation officer or the CEO.

The Benefits of Internal Crowdsourcing

Companies that employ external crowdsourcing need to confront several issues.[4] First, because many of the crowd participants aren't specifically familiar with the organization or the context in which it operates, a high percentage of the suggestions may not be easy to implement. The voice of the customer obtained through external crowdsourcing may be very good at describing the pain points and needs but not necessarily good at figuring out how to solve the problems. Indeed, proposals often call for strategic assets that companies don't have and can't afford. What's more, external crowdsourcing can stir up intellectual property issues involving who owns the ideas.[5]

While internal crowds are typically not as diverse as external crowds (and therefore less apt to propose radically new ideas), they have more localized knowledge. This can help companies turn suggestions into workable actions better and faster. Employees, especially people working on the front lines, often have intimate knowledge about the kinds of changes that are feasible, given the company's circumstances and current assets. Many of the solutions can be formulated as patches and workarounds to satisfy particular needs, and solutions obtained through internal crowdsourcing can have a rapid impact in the marketplace. In addition, the intellectual property issues tend to be less complicated because employees, rather than outsiders, are the ones providing the ideas.

Internal crowdsourcing events enable employees to express their ideas. By organizing these events, companies can send the important message to employees that their knowledge is valuable and the company depends on it. With mechanisms to share their views and structure internal collaboration, employees

Where Is the Crowd?

Outside the company	Inside the company
Hidden benefit: *Creating marketing buzz*	Hidden benefit: *Employee engagement*

Implementability of solutions

Ease of handling intellectual property issues

Overcoming "not invented here" syndrome

Organizational learning and knowledge diffusion

Advantages of internal crowds

Diversity of ideas

Direct engagement with customers

Implicit customer feedback on solutions

Increased marketability of solutions

Advantages of external crowds

Comparing the Benefits of Internal vs. External Crowds

While internal crowds are typically not as diverse as external crowds, the solutions employees propose may be more readily implemented and can have a rapid impact in the marketplace.

can feel empowered and engaged in the company's innovation efforts. Research shows that employees working in collaborative environments tend to be more satisfied with the innovation process.[6] This can lead to higher employee morale and lower turnover.[7]

Roadblocks to Successful Internal Crowdsourcing

As fruitful as internal crowdsourcing can be, it's common for companies to hit roadblocks in reaping the full potential of internal crowds. In the course of our research, we have identified seven barriers that involve participation, collaboration, and implementation. They are:

- Rather than encourage employees to think broadly and creatively, companies often ask employees to concentrate on incremental adjustments to processes and on improving existing products and services. In doing so, many employees become confused about the purpose of internal crowdsourcing and how it's different from other initiatives in the company, such as continuous quality improvement and business process reengineering.

- Given their other work responsibilities, many employees don't have time to participate in crowdsourcing activities.

- Employees may be hesitant to participate, particularly when managers and internal experts are part of the mix and are using their real identities. This dynamic may crowd out people who have knowledge that can lead to innovative solutions or who want to develop solutions by working with others in the crowd.

- Most companies run their crowdsourcing initiatives using a competitive process. Rather than encouraging participants to work with others to create solutions together, some companies distribute rewards based on the ideas submitted by individuals.

- Sometimes, the technology platforms themselves focus people on contributing ideas and not on developing solutions together.
- After crowdsourcing events end, employees don't always receive sufficient information on what happened to ideas.
- Over and above the lack of feedback, those who suggest solutions don't always get opportunities to develop their ideas into solutions.

Removing the Roadblocks

In response to the roadblocks we have noted above, we have developed a set of seven action steps to help executives make their internal crowdsourcing efforts more effective. The first four steps should be considered either before or during a crowdsourcing event; the others are used once the event has occurred.

Keep the focus on innovation. It may be tempting to use internal crowdsourcing events to solicit ideas about short-term improvements. However, to get the most out of internal crowdsourcing, companies should resist this impulse and encourage employees to keep their focus on long-term opportunities. A large research and development (R&D) company we studied, for example, announced that it wanted employees to identify products and services that would be feasible in 2025. This encouraged employees to think more broadly than usual.

Other companies have defined challenges in a more open-ended way. A US telecom infrastructure products and services provider presented its employees with a general question: "What are some strategies for our company to transition to a services-centric business to address new markets and new customers?" How questions are framed is a critical component of signaling and can influence how employees approach internal crowdsourcing initiatives.

Another critical aspect of establishing the grounds for creativity is to share with crowdsourcing participants the criteria that will be used to filter and select the best solutions. For example, an R&D-intensive company we studied disclosed the following parameters that its executives planned to use for selecting solutions: 50% would be weighted on crowd voting, 30% on novelty of the idea, and 20% on the potential to create new businesses. Fashion and retail company Li & Fung Ltd., based in Hong Kong, told employees that solutions from internal crowdsourcing would be picked based on six criteria: (1) ability to meet customers' unmet needs, (2) delighting the customer, (3) the solution's newness, (4) marketability, (5) commercial viability, and (6) scalability.

Give internal crowdsourcing participants slack time. One of the main reasons people participate in external crowdsourcing events is to have fun.[8] However, a critical difference between external and internal crowdsourcing is that many employees, particularly frontline employees, have very little discretionary time to participate. A managed health care company came up with a smart way to engage internal employees without undermining existing schedules. It notified supervisors of proposed dates for internal crowdsourcing events and asked them to select days when they could give employees some downtime. Once the dates were set, supervisors encouraged employees to participate in the internal crowdsourcing innovation challenges. We found that offering employees slack time to participate in internal crowdsourcing events can be a key factor in making the events successful, especially when the companies want the employees to work together to develop new solutions. When done well, internal crowdsourcing challenges not only produce ideas but also engage employees in a learning process.

Allow for anonymous participation. Difficulties can occur when participants in internal crowdsourcing use their organizational identities. Rather than freely promoting ideas that address the issues at hand, some individuals may feel compelled to defend their formal positions. Internal crowdsourcing participants should feel safe about contributing knowledge, regardless of their seniority or role in the company. One way to encourage this is to offer a degree of anonymity. Several of the companies we studied allowed employees to contribute their ideas anonymously, freeing them up to share knowledge that they might have kept to themselves if they felt pressured to advocate on behalf of the units they represented. Providing a psychologically safe environment leads to greater employee participation and collaboration, resulting in more effective innovations.[9] At Li & Fung, for example, almost 90% of the solutions the company received through internal crowdsourcing challenges were from junior to mid-level employees, and about 30% of the solutions were proposed by people working in support functions such as human resources, IT, and finance.

Participants who are forced to use their real names often feel exposed during internal crowdsourcing challenges, especially if they are recognized internally as subject matter experts. With anonymity, they don't have to worry about how their ideas "look." This allows them to focus on learning and integrating the knowledge being shared.

Take steps to ensure that company experts don't exert their influence too heavily. Experts within a company may be inclined to wield their knowledge during the idea generation process, and this can be harmful. Although the voices of experts are often valuable, they can intimidate others in the company, who worry that they are out of place expressing ideas to a crowd that includes experts.

For internal crowdsourcing to produce innovative outcomes, efforts should be made to keep the process open to diverse perspectives. At an R&D-intensive company, the managers in charge of an internal crowdsourcing effort initially prohibited R&D employees from participating in a crowdsourcing event. The company changed its position when participants asked to see research evidence related to the question they were considering and specifically asked if they could hear from R&D experts.

A US manufacturer, by contrast, determined that internal crowdsourcing participation by internal experts could be a strong plus. For its crowdsourcing initiative, the company asked some internal experts to serve as the moderators of crowd discussions. This involved teeing up questions to challenge the crowd to think of different ways to create new solutions. Among the questions the expert moderators asked: How could the idea be extended in new ways? How could we combine it with another idea? How could we differentiate it from other products on the market? How could we adapt the product to a different target audience?

There are benefits to both approaches. However, the decision to involve internal experts has a downside as well as an upside. Companies need to recognize that internal experts are often motivated to promote their own ideas. However, participants need to know that their suggestions will be highly valued. When engaging experts in an internal crowdsourcing event, companies should train them to operate as moderators and to do what they can to encourage others.

Use a collaborative process for internal crowdsourcing. One of the secrets to unlocking the creative potential of internal crowds is recognizing that the goal isn't simply to generate winning ideas. It's also to build a system through which people within the organization share knowledge, learn from one another, and offer pertinent knowledge for use in new solutions.

We saw companies use one or both steps of a two-step process to foster collaboration in internal crowdsourcing innovation challenges. First, they asked people to share pertinent knowledge related to innovation opportunities. The emphasis here was on broad employee participation: asking people to share facts, examples, trade-offs, and even wild ideas. Then the companies asked people to help shape the knowledge into comprehensive solutions. The majority of the companies we studied relied heavily on the second approach.

However, some companies find it useful to use a hybrid, multistage approach whereby in initial stages the internal crowd shares raw ideas through a technology platform. Then, in the later stages, ad hoc teams are formed to pursue the most promising ideas further and develop them into comprehensive solutions. For example, Li & Fung asked employees from around the world to submit their ideas via a web-based platform. After that, a team of executives and internal experts selected the most promising ideas, based on preestablished criteria. Employees had opportunities to vote on the best ideas, narrowing the selections down to eight. In the final stage, teams composed of the idea originators and others who helped refine the ideas presented the solutions to a senior team that oversaw the internal crowdsourcing challenge. The top three teams were then asked to refine their solutions before traveling to corporate headquarters to present to a broader set of executives.

Companies that use a multistage process should provide incentives so that employees feel it's worth their while to follow the process and support the overall goal. If rewards go only to people who propose solid ideas, there can be negative consequences. People with half-baked ideas will submit them in hopes of winning, but those who don't have solid ideas (but might have input that could conceivably lead to important ideas) will hesitate to share their knowledge without incentives to do so. On the other hand, if incentives are offered only to good collaborators, there won't be incentives to contribute initial ideas that can lead to the development of comprehensive solutions. For these reasons, most of the companies we studied that succeeded with internal crowdsourcing offered different types of incentives. For example, a large industrial products company offered modest rewards ($50 gift cards) to both top idea contributors and collaborators. Top collaborators were determined by aggregating points for contributing new ideas, commenting on and refining other people's ideas, and combining multiple ideas into more robust solutions. They also received points based on their voting on other people's ideas.

We found that many participants lacked the time to engage fully in innovation activities. Instead, they logged on to the platform, took part in an innovation activity if it was easy to do so, and then left. We also found that crowd members responded in different ways to internal crowdsourcing platforms. Some responded to outcome-based incentives; others responded to process-based incentives. Regardless of how companies structure their internal crowdsourcing process, executives should remember that processes and incentives drive behavior.

Design platforms that facilitate shared development and evolution of solutions. Currently, there are a number of platforms available for crowdsourcing. Ironically, the technology platforms that are intended to help companies use internal crowdsourcing can cause roadblocks. In many cases, the platform makes it easy only for participants to submit their own ideas; it does little to connect individuals with ideas from other participants. The inability to see what other participants are suggesting can be a barrier to collaboration. Even if the platform allows for knowledge to be visible by others, it may allow for only limited interaction (for example, commenting or voting on others' contributions). Internal crowdsourcing platforms that support more innovative solutions use an implicit multistage process. The platforms encourage crowds to share knowledge (such as how other companies or other industries have solved similar problems) and then work that information into creative solutions. In particular, there are three features that we believe foster creativity in internal crowdsourcing: (1) knowledge sharing among the crowd across a variety of knowledge types (not just ideas); (2) the opportunity for coevolution of solutions by the crowd; and (3) the degree to which feedback from the crowd helps to refine ideas.

With these features in mind, we studied how companies used platforms to foster innovation in internal crowdsourcing challenges. The most popular platforms were online discussion forums and idea suggestion systems. When executives charged with innovation sought to engage individuals, they tended to use one of these platforms. However, such platforms do not explicitly encourage processes for groups to collaborate to create solutions together. Rather, they encourage individuals to post their ideas in the hope that other people will come in and refine the ideas. Although ideas can be refined after they have been posted, the platforms aren't designed to support and promote members of the crowd sharing knowledge that's relevant to the innovation opportunity. Online discussion forums also don't tend to make it easy for crowds to collaboratively piece together knowledge; even if some of the raw ideas have innovation potential, companies often need to wait until after the crowdsourcing event to sift through all the contributions, collect the innovation nuggets, and then work the ideas into comprehensive solutions. This postcrowdsourcing process can be onerous (particularly if the crowd generates thousands of potential innovation ideas). Given the time constraints and executives' predilections for picking solutions that leverage existing assets and capabilities, the executives in charge of sifting through and combining the ideas posted by the crowd may settle for less than optimal solutions.

While many companies use idea suggestion systems and online discussion forums, we found that some companies utilize cocreation platforms as a way to encourage greater crowd engagement and produce more innovative solutions from internal crowds. Such platforms explicitly encourage activities that go beyond the rudimentary activities of idea posting, commenting, and selecting. Typically, the first stage encourages people to share knowledge based on their rich and diverse experiences. This may include providing: (1) facts and established practices relevant to the opportunity; (2) examples of how other companies have addressed similar opportunities; (3) preliminary ideas that other people might build upon; and (4) insights about how to approach trade-offs not as compromises but as opportunities for innovation. The second stage then encourages people to integrate the knowledge into coherent solutions.

Be transparent about plans for follow-up postcrowdsourcing. Once employees have participated in internal crowdsourcing events, they want to know about the results. Which ideas were selected for further development and why? Will people be asked to develop some of the solutions more fully? Companies need to have procedures for how crowdsourcing suggestions are handled. At the managed health care company, for example, the executives pledged to send out a detailed review of the crowd recommendations within one week of the completion of the internal crowdsourcing event. The project team committed to sending an email to all participants both announcing the winners and describing how the team planned to move ideas forward.

It's common for employees to be curious about how the ideas they submit are being viewed—and more specifically, who "owns" the solutions. In several settings, we found that crowdsourcing participants wanted to play a role in prototyping, testing, and implementing the ideas they proposed. A large international software company responds to this type of interest by inviting members of winning teams (both the initial proposers and collaborators) to participate in implementation efforts.

To maintain interest among employees whose suggested solutions are not selected for further development, companies should work to establish an atmosphere of openness and fairness. This can include providing opportunities for people to submit solutions more than once. One telecom company, for example, encourages employees whose solutions were not selected in the initial round to resubmit the ideas for consideration. The senior executive in charge of internal crowdsourcing sees this as a way to encourage participation and to demonstrate fairness.

Another way to demonstrate fairness is to commit to providing substantive feedback to employees who suggest solutions that are not chosen. Although companies are accustomed to giving recognition to teams who submit winning solutions, they don't always offer clear criteria to guide the process or take the time to follow up with employees who don't win. But these efforts can pay big dividends in terms of driving future participation and generating better solutions later on. If internal crowdsourcing is to become an important mechanism for the organization's ongoing renewal, management needs to be serious about offering feedback.

In general, because roadblocks can surface at different points in the internal crowdsourcing process, the activity needs to be actively managed to ensure high levels of employee participation. However, it may be well worth the investment. The potential benefits of greater employee engagement are significant. A senior manager at an e-commerce solutions provider, for example, told us that during a 10-day crowdsourcing challenge, employees proposed more than 100 new solutions. Moreover, companies such as Li & Fung have noted that the level of employee participation in internal crowdsourcing events often goes well beyond what other collaboration mechanisms (such as virtual teams, face-to-face brainstorming, and innovation workshops) achieve. Despite its challenges, internal crowdsourcing can be used to unlock a company's innovation potential.

Notes

1. L. Myler, "AT&T's Innovation Pipeline Engages 130,000 Employees," December 5, 2013, https://www.forbes.com/sites/larrymyler/2013/12 /05/atts-innovation-pipeline-engages-130000-employees; A. Ivanov, "Crowdsourcing vs. Employees: How to Benefit from Both," April 4, 2012, https://www.cmswire.com/cms/social-business/crowdsourcing-vs-employees-how-to-benefit-from-both-015083.php; R. Moussavian, "Work 4.0 Put in Practice," August 24, 2016, https://www.telekom.com/ en/company/management-unplugged/details/work-4-0-put-in-practice-436002; and R. Singel, "Google Taps Employees to Crowdsource Its Venture Capital Arm," May 3, 2010, https://www.wired.com/2010/05 /google-ventures.

2. E. Bonabeau, "Decisions 2.0: The Power of Collective Intelligence," *MIT Sloan Management Review* 50, no. 2 (2009): 45–52; and K. J. Boudreau and K. R. Lakhani, "Using the Crowd as an Innovation Partner," *Harvard Business Review* 91, no. 4 (2013): 60–69.

3. A. Siegel, "How Internal Crowdsourcing Will Transform the Way We Do Business," March 11, 2016, https://www.business2community.com/ business-innovation/internal-crowdsourcing-will-transform-way-business-01475798; and H. Balmaekers, "The Crowd Within—Crowd-sourced Innovation Inside Companies," March 23, 2016, https:// innov8rs.co/news/crowd-within-crowdsourced-innovation-inside-companies.

4. A. Majchrzak and A. Malhotra, "Towards an Information Systems Perspective and Research Agenda on Crowdsourcing for Innovation," *Journal of Strategic Information Systems* 22, no. 4 (2013): 257–268; and A. Malhotra and A. Majchrzak, "Managing Crowds in Innovation Challenges," *California Management Review* 56, no. 4 (2014): 103–123.

5. M. Lieberstein and A. Tucker, "Crowdsourcing and Intellectual Property Issues," Association of Corporate Counsel, August 29, 2012, http:// www.acc.com/legalresources/quickcounsel/caipi.cfm.

6. S. G. Scott and R. A. Bruce, "Determinants of Innovative Behavior: A Path Model of Individual Innovation in the Workplace," *Academy of Management Journal* 37, no. 3 (1994): 580–607.

7. J. Baldoni, "Employee Engagement Does More Than Boost Productivity," *Harvard Business Review*, July 4, 2013, https://hbr.org/2013/07/employee-engagement-does-more.

8. D. C. Brabham, "Moving the Crowd at iStockphoto: The Composition of the Crowd and Motivations for Participation in a Crowdsourcing Application," *First Monday* 13, no. 6 (2008): http://firstmonday.org/article/view/2159/1969.

9. M. Baer and M. Frese, "Innovation Is Not Enough: Climates for Initiative and Psychological Safety, Process Innovations, and Firm Performance," *Journal of Organizational Behavior* 24, no. 1 (2003): 45–68; M. A. West and W. M. M. Altink, "Innovation at Work: Individual, Group, Organizational, and Socio-Historical Perspectives," *European Journal of Work and Organizational Psychology* 5, no. 1 (1996): 3–11; and F. Yuan and R. W. Woodman, "Innovative Behavior in the Workplace: The Role of Performance and Image Outcome Expectations," *Academy of Management Journal* 53, no. 2 (2010): 323–342.

4

Collaborating with Customer Communities: Lessons from the Lego Group

Yun Mi Antorini, Albert M. Muñiz Jr., and Tormod Askildsen

Customer-oriented companies pride themselves on their ability to understand the experiences and insights of the marketplace and then integrate the best ideas into future products.[1] But what would it be like if you found that you had hundreds, if not thousands, of knowledgeable users of your products ready and eager to spend nights and weekends acting as extensions of your research and development department? For the Lego Group, a maker of children's creative construction toys based in Billund, Denmark, this close bond with the user community—not just children but a large coterie of adults who have been using its products for years—is not a pipe dream but a reality.

Lego users have a long tradition of innovation and sharing their innovations with one another—activities that the internet has made much easier. As Lego managers became more aware of innovations by the company's adult fans, the managers realized that at least some of the adult fans' ideas would be interesting to the company's core target market of children. In 2005, Lego created the Ambassador Program to provide a fast and direct way for the company and its fans to get into contact with one another. The program has provided considerable value to both sides.

- For the Lego Group, the program has offered exposure to new ideas, new technologies, and new business partnerships. Management saw that not everything needed to be developed internally. Indeed, the company has found ways to expand into new market areas without having to sustain long-term fixed costs.

- For the adult fans, collaborations have allowed them to influence Lego's business decisions and encourage the company to develop products targeting teens and adults. In some cases, Lego has decided to back businesses that produce products related to its own.

Through trial and error, Lego has developed a solid understanding of what it takes to build and maintain profitable and mutually beneficial collaborations with users. In what follows, we will examine the emergence of Lego's user communities, how management's involvement with user groups has evolved, and the core principles that Lego has formulated for successful interaction with its user groups.

About the Research

Between 2003 and 2011, we engaged in a multisite research program to examine community development and user innovation among adult fans of Lego and to learn about Lego's experiences and practices in working with external communities. We participated in eight conventions in North America, Denmark, and Germany. The conventions were attended by between 50 and 400 adult fans, who displayed their innovations and took part in presentations, workshops, competitions, auctions, and roundtable discussions. We also observed adult users at smaller and locally arranged events such as visits to the Lego offices and the Legoland park in Billund, Denmark; monthly Lego user group meetings; and Lego shopping trips. In total, we conducted 85 hours of observation, which we consolidated into 180 pages of field notes; recorded two hours of video and shot and collected 454 photos; and maintained a file that included physical materials produced by Lego fans (including event programs, event T-shirts, name tags, posters, and magazines). We also closely followed adult Lego users on community forums and sites and collected profiles that members uploaded on Lugnet.com, the Lego User Group Network. The forums addressed community membership, Lego hobby activities and tastes, and practices related to adult Lego users' innovations. In total, we amassed 1,016 pages of double-spaced text.

In addition, we conducted 25 in-depth interviews and several informal interviews with members of the community, face to face or via email or phone. Face-to-face and phone interviews typically lasted between one and two hours. During the research process, the lead author became a member of the Danish Lego User Group and made presentations and led roundtable discussions at North American adult user conventions. Many of the findings presented in this paper have been previously shared with adult users at community events and online forums, thus offering the community opportunities to comment on the findings and conclusions.

Finally, we collected data on community web pages where Lego employees communicated with users and text from Lego.com and user community sites regarding the Lego Ambassador Program. This data helped us describe the user community and what ties members together; user innovations and the needs they serve; and what Lego has learned.

The Emergence of Lego User Communities

For decades, Lego's colorful plastic bricks were developed for and used by children who played alone or with a few playmates. As the children grew up, they generally outgrew their interest in Lego products. However, beginning in the late 1990s, two things happened: The company introduced a series of new products that appealed to older users, such as Lego *Star Wars* and Lego Mindstorms; and the internet enabled people to connect in completely new ways, prompting many adults to return to Lego play and transform their play experiences into a serious and demanding adult hobby. By 1999, there were 11 known Lego user groups, mainly located in North America. By 2006, the trend had expanded globally to include more than 60 groups. And by February 2012, there were more than 150 known user groups, with over 100,000 active adult fans worldwide.

In developing innovations, adult Lego users tap into a deep understanding and knowledge of the company's product line, its possibilities and its limitations. For example, they have developed completely new strategy games, new modular building standards, and specialized software. These user-created innovations have expanded the Lego play experience and pushed the use of Lego materials into new and virtual media, enabling creative possibilities that weren't previously possible. The innovations have created value for the innovator and encouraged deeper community engagement and community vitality.[2]

Consider, for example, a service innovation called Auczilla that was introduced in 1995. It enabled people (often adult fans) to buy specific (often huge) quantities of Lego pieces online. Auczilla's successor, BrickLink, which began in 2000, sells pieces through more than 5,800 online shops. The largest secondary marketplace for Lego sets and elements, it recently had about 200,000 registered members and offers more than 134 million Lego elements for sale.

Adult fans also pioneered more advanced ways of designing Lego models. An early example of this was LDraw, a freeware computer-aided design program released in 1995. The program allowed computer users to develop, test, render, and document designs based on Lego parts before constructing the models and sharing the designs, much the way architects and industrial designers rely on CAD professionally. Although the developer, James Jessiman, died in 1997, LDraw's impact on the Lego community endures. Tools are available today for Windows, Macintosh, and Linux operating systems. LDraw allows users to export and import Lego parts lists from their designs to online shops listed on the BrickLink site, enabling them to identify and order the exact elements they need to create their models.

Adult fans have also created hundreds of minor improvements that make the play experience more inspiring, fun, and challenging for them and fellow users. For example, user innovations made it possible to customize Lego Minifigures, build themes that better mirror personal interests, and combine Lego pieces in new ways to make unique expressions and functions.

Many of the fan innovations have improved and extended the Lego building system or introduced new ways to use it that dovetailed well with how Lego itself thought of its products. Over the years, adult fans have uploaded more than 300,000 of their own Lego creations on MOCpages.com (one of the many sites fans use for sharing their work) and posted more than 4.5 million photos, drawings, and instructions online. In addition, fans have shared thousands of Lego-inspired movies on You-Tube, with the top five movies attracting more than 64 million views. Cumulatively, the fan activity represents a vast library of free ideas available to anyone.

How Lego's Relationship with User Groups Has Evolved

Historically, Lego was an extremely private company that tightly controlled its products and intellectual property. The company's public position was "We don't accept unsolicited ideas." However, things began to change in the late 1990s following the introduction of a new line of kits called Lego Mindstorms, which contained software and hardware to create small customizable and programmable robots. Sophisticated users found ways to hack into the code and adapt the new products; they talked about their innovations on independent websites. This presented Lego management with a choice: either pursue legal action against the hackers or invite users to collaborate on new products and applications. The company concluded that litigation would be difficult and costly—and also that there could be significant advantages to collaborating with users.

Among Lego employees, there was skepticism about how collaboration with adult users would actually work. After all, many of the adult users didn't know or care about designing products for the company's target market—children. To make things simple, the company put a small team of Lego employees in charge of reviewing fan input to make sure that it was properly aligned with the company's marketing goals. This internal "sign off" was in place for several years. Meanwhile, Lego experienced a turbulent period from 1998 to 2004 (unrelated to its involvement with the user community), characterized by escalating competitive pressures and financial losses.

The appointment of a new CEO, Jørgen Vig Knudstorp, in 2004 provided the opportunity for Lego to reflect on the meaning of the brand as well as the value of the company's ties with the user community. Knudstorp, who joined the company in 2001, concluded rather quickly that the benefits of collaboration were unmistakable. "We think innovation will come from a dialogue with the community," he told a North American user convention in 2005. This marked the beginning of a new push for openness and collaboration—and innovative products built around the Lego elements.

About the same time that Knudstorp became CEO, more senior managers began realizing that while many of the innovations adult users initiated were beyond the *design* capabilities of children, they were not necessarily beyond a child's *adoption* capability. For example, vice president (then marketing director) Søren Lund recalled working closely with a community liaison to get adult fans to contribute to the design of the Lego Factory sets that were introduced in 2005. "Our intention was to make it as much of a community project as possible," Lund noted.[3] They began in March 2004 by selecting an adult fan team leader, who set up a secure forum where users could share their designs. In the space of a few short weeks, the level of fan activity was tremendous, Lund noted, adding, "I was overwhelmed by the quality." The success of this project "sent shock waves through our development organization."

Since then, Lego has formalized relationships with the adult fan community through its Ambassador Program. Representatives, drawn from across the community of Lego user groups, provide a fast and direct way for Lego managers to get in contact with adult fans who may have new product or marketing ideas or be interested in providing feedback on products currently in development.

Lego's relationship with user groups and fans offers significant benefits. Not only do fans inject energy and ideas, but in some cases they help refocus products. For example, during the development of a new version of the Lego Mindstorms programmable robotics kit in 2004, tech-savvy users advised management that the new product would provide many more design opportunities if it worked with a larger selection of sensors. It turned out that one of the users who participated on the development team, John Barnes, was in the business of manufacturing high-tech sensors. By partnering with Barnes' company, Lego was able to offer 12 different types of advanced sensors with Mindstorms

NXT, which greatly expanded its capabilities over prior models. Although the sensors were designed and manufactured by Barnes' company, they were marketed through the Lego online shop, making them the first components dedicated to a Lego product to be manufactured by an independent vendor. Without Barnes' involvement, it is unlikely that Lego would have been able to create a profitable business case for the development and sales of the additional sensors.

Similarly, adult fans have helped Lego identify new product lines and distribution strategies, including one new line featuring models of architecturally significant buildings. In developing these products, the company worked closely with Chicago architect and Lego enthusiast Adam Reed Tucker to represent such structures as the Empire State Building, the White House, the Brandenburg Gate, and Frank Lloyd Wright's landmark Fallingwater residence in Pennsylvania. After a pilot of the new line was conducted in Chicago, the architectural kits are now sold around the world in outlets such as museums, souvenir shops, and bookstores.

Based on its experience working with dedicated users, Lego management has developed an informed view on the circumstances under which collaborating closely with users works well—and on when it doesn't.

When It Works Well

Lego management has found collaboration to be most successful when outside parties have a particular area of expertise, such as architecture or sensor design and manufacture, that individuals within the company don't have. Other reasons to consider partnering are when the target market is too small or a partner's cost structure is much lower (as was the case with the electronic sensors). In such circumstances, Lego has benefited from having passionate fans with deep and specialized knowledge of Lego building along with their own specific expertise. Since many new products fail, having innovations that can be pretested by potential customers helps eliminate bugs and reduce risk.

Cocreating knowledge-intensive innovations with users allows Lego to obtain the skills and knowledge important to these activities. In addition to ad hoc collaborations, in recent years Lego has hired more than 20 adult fans. By hiring experienced users, Lego can benefit from the extensive knowledge and skills these users have accumulated over the years.

When It Causes Difficulties

Collaborating with users has turned out to be less successful in cases where users seek to push the products beyond their intended limits. To achieve extraordinary results, adult Lego fans sometimes promote building techniques that go beyond the parameters of what the products were designed for. From Lego's perspective, the concern is that while many of these techniques add quite stunning expressions and functions, they challenge quality and in most cases are too hard for younger users to build. Whereas the primary end users from Lego's perspective are children, adult fans often think about developing products for other adults.

Core Principles for Successful Interaction with Users

Based on its experiences working with the user community, Lego has developed a set of principles that summarize what it has learned about collaborating and interacting with knowledgeable users.

Be clear about rules and expectations. Without exception, the adult users who collaborate with the Lego Group have busy lives that involve full-time jobs, studies, hobbies, families, and so on. When Lego began collaborating with adult fans, there were very few stated rules or expectations about how the process should work. This led to frustrations on both sides. Fans complained about being asked to consider cost and complexity when developing their designs and to adhere to building techniques that met the company's tight quality and safety standards. Lego employees complained that adult fans pushed the limits of the company's rules and regulations and that coordination was difficult because most of the adult fans had full-time jobs and worked on their Lego projects after business hours, at night. Lego learned that it had to be more specific about its expectations upfront, including when its projects would begin and end. The company also learned that adult users were more cooperative when they negotiated expectations with the Lego employees directly involved, rather than with Lego managers who were not directly engaged in the work.

Ensure a win-win. In collaborating with very engaged and skilled users who were contributing their ideas, it was easy for the company to focus on "getting the job done," forgetting that the users had needs that sometimes diverged from those of Lego employees and that the collaborations themselves needed to be rewarding experiences for the users. Developing a win-win mind-set must be a priority. Lego management learned, as studies of innovators have found, that the intrinsic rewards associated with designing and building products are frequently more motivating than financial rewards.[4] Recognizing this, Lego has tended to pay outside collaborators with a combination of experience, access, and Lego products. However, users who participate in long-term projects or who provide services that are more like "work" are given a choice: they can receive free products or a more conventional stipend. In business partnerships between Lego and users (for example, in cases such as the architecture project and the sensors), various long-term, fee-based partnership agreements have been negotiated.

Recognize that outsiders aren't insiders. Lego employees involved with the user community learned early in the process that while participants were indeed committed to the Lego brand and the Lego brick, they were also attracted to the sense of community they experienced with other adult fans. In fact, it is the relationship with other fans and the input and encouragement they offer that strongly motivate these users to keep raising the creative bar and keep searching for new and better ideas and solutions. User communities are not just extensions of the company—they are independent entities. As a result, members should be treated as passionate, experienced, and talented individuals.

Don't expect one size to fit all. Lego also learned early on that different users prefer different modes of communication, and different types of innovations call for different environments. As a result, Lego relies on many different collaboration platforms. The simplest are polls and electronic idea boxes, which allow users to give input on predefined topics. A more advanced platform, Lego Digital Designer, allows users to design virtual Lego models and create digital building instructions that can be shared with other users. It allows innovators with different skill levels to participate.

A newer platform, Lego Cuusoo, allows users to upload designs (drawings, photos, etc.) to a web page where other Lego users and consumers in general can vote on the design.[5] If a design receives 10,000 votes, Lego agrees to consider it for possible production; if the design is commercialized, innovators receive 1% of the total net sales for their product. In 2011, the Minecraft project received 10,000 votes worldwide within 48 hours.[6] It has also received 30,000 "likes" on the Lego and Minecraft Facebook pages and was tweeted about more than 4,000 times.

Finally, the company shapes new ideas through user panels and virtual project rooms. Typically, these restricted forums gather input from very skilled users on complex, long-term projects. For example, hundreds of beta test users proposed improvements to and reported flaws in the Lego Mindstorms NXT, and several thousand user posts appeared in the virtual project room for Lego's Hobby Train set.

Be as open as possible. To protect confidential and proprietary information, companies customarily ask collaborators to sign nondisclosure agreements. That's what Lego did when it launched its Lego Ambassador Program and began collaborating with adult fans. Lego learned two important things: NDAs were effective at preventing the collaborators from sharing information with third parties, but there were unintended consequences. Because Ambassadors took the NDAs seriously, they didn't share their ideas with other adult fans who hadn't signed NDAs. Today, Lego uses NDAs more sparingly, to limit information sharing with third parties only in narrowly defined situations— thus ensuring that collaborators are able to interact with each other to the maximum extent. Lego also attempts to maintain transparency in all matters related to collaboration. For example, it posts detailed descriptions of the criteria for and responsibilities of Lego Ambassadors on its own home page and on several community websites. And the company supports community initiatives aimed at improving idea sharing among community members and advancing innovation.

Cumulatively, the principles we have discussed here help Lego organize collaborations with users in a manner that balances the needs of the company with those of its users. These lessons are applicable to other organizations. Instead of regarding collaboration as something that needs to be managed exclusively by the company, it is fruitful to think of it as an ongoing dialogue between two allies. Both sides contribute important resources to a common purpose. Frequently, the two sets of resources complement each other and advance the conversation and collaboration.

The authors thank Eric von Hippel for his valuable feedback on this article. Also, the authors thank Paal Smith-Meyer and his colleagues in the Lego New Business Group, and the many Lego enthusiasts who over the years have shared their knowledge and insights with us.

Notes

1. P. Gloor and S. Cooper, "The New Principles of a Swarm Business," *MIT Sloan Management Review* 48, no. 3 (2007): 81–84.
2. Y. M. Antorini and A. M. Muñiz Jr., "Self-Extension, Brand Community, and User Innovation," in *The Routledge Companion to Identity and Consumption* (Abingdon, UK: Routledge, 2012); and H. J. Schau, A. M. Muñiz Jr., and E. J. Arnould, "How Brand Community Practices Create Value," *Journal of Marketing* 73, no. 5 (2009): 30–51.
3. J. McKee, "Behind the Curtains—Lego Factory AFOL Project Team," November 16, 2004, http://www.lugnet.cc/lego/?n=2588.

4. N. Franke and S. Shah, "How Communities Support Innovative Activities: An Exploration of Assistance and Sharing Among End-users," *Research Policy* 32, no. 1 (2003): 157–78.
5. Cuusoo in Japanese means "imagination" or "wish."
6. The Lego Cuusoo blog, December 8, 2011, http://legocuusoo.posterous.com.

II

Strategic Perspectives

5

Finding a Lower-Risk Path to High-Impact Innovations

Joseph V. Sinfield and Freddy Solis

When people talk about innovation, they often envision the big technical or conceptual advances that change the way we live—developments that have profound and lasting impact. Corning Inc.'s research in low-loss fused silica in the 1970s, which paved the way for breakthroughs in fiber-optic communications, sensing, and imaging applications, falls into this category. Early research by the US Defense Advanced Research Projects Agency (DARPA), which established the foundations of machine-to-machine communication protocols and the internet, clearly does too. Another example is the technique of crowdsourcing, which has spawned dramatic and previously unimagined solutions to business and technical challenges (for example, the National Aeronautics and Space Administration's [NASA's] Citizen Science, Kiva's crowdfunding platform, or Foldit, the online game about protein folding).

Stories of foundational investments that unleashed enduring growth for major companies have been etched into our business lore. Procter & Gamble Co.'s investments in science, for example, led to the formulation of Tide and other synthetic detergents as well as mass-produced diapers. E. I. du Pont & Nemours & Co.'s early investments in synthetic fibers and polymers (which were considered highly uncertain at the time) led to the development of nylon and Teflon. For Procter & Gamble and DuPont, the innovations have spurred decades of growth and opened doors to an array of related businesses, while also generating beneficial impacts for their customers.

However, significant innovation breakthroughs are rare occurrences in most domains. In addition to being perceived as difficult (and costly) to orchestrate, pursuing breakthrough innovation is widely seen as extremely risky. In fact, in a number of industries, including pharmaceuticals and petrochemicals, tolerance for risk taking has fallen sharply in recent years. For several reasons, including near-term investor pressures, a tendency to "stick to what we know," and concerns about general market volatility, making big bets on breakthrough innovations has become more difficult to justify.

The Risk–Return Paradox

The perception of risk that underlies these trends is founded in classical risk–return doctrine.[1] Innovation initiatives and the funding programs that support them are generally viewed as "investments," with an expectation that taking higher risks should be rewarded with higher returns. At the low-risk, low-return end of the spectrum, we tend to see investments that drive incremental innovation or development of innovations that are already proven. At the opposite extreme are corporate "skunk works" that seek to drive innovation in technology and business models to develop whole new product or service categories. Similarly, programs such as DARPA, which finance a portfolio of blue-sky initiatives, offer no guarantees that any particular innovation will pay off. But if such initiatives are successful, they can create widespread benefits for society.[2]

The accepted wisdom involving risk and return has led many to assume that high returns must be accompanied by high risk, while low-risk innovations tend to involve low returns. This leaves a notable void: a zone of investments that offer lower risk and high return. Our research suggests that this zone is not a null set, particularly when "return" is reframed as "positive impact," both for the organization pursuing the innovation and for others, and when focus is placed not only on the investment itself but also on how it is pursued. The link between financial results and impact stems from user adoption, which can be accelerated through broader engagement with a new idea. We recognize that this notion is counterintuitive. Indeed, some might argue that successful innovation "moonshots" are the results of serendipity, risk taking, and a long evolutionary process. However, based on what we learned from a number of cases in our research, the risk of a high-impact effort stems not only from the ambitious nature of the goals but also from the way goals are framed and pursued. In this chapter, we examine a proactive and comparatively less risky approach to pursuing high-impact innovation—one that strings together "lily pads" of capability-building investments, technical and conceptual advances, and market explorations into what we call *enabling innovations*.[3]

About the Research

We pursued three research streams that were iteratively triangulated over the course of five years. First, we tried to integrate seemingly disparate insights within and across perspectives and disciplines related to the challenge of innovating with high impact. We examined bodies of literature that are relevant to high-impact innovations, including management, design, entrepreneurism, systems, and learning, with the goal of placing specialized high-impact innovation knowledge into a broader context. Included in this generative synthesis were perspectives found across the policy, design, economics, and history of science bodies of knowledge, as well as research and reports from nongovernmental organizations that were used to characterize impact and define its links to innovation.

Second, we did a qualitative study of secondary research sources that documented the history of high-impact innovations using a technique called thematic analysis. We analyzed these historical case examples, which ranged from the development of lasers to the evolution of microfinance, to identify patterns of innovation impact across situations that spanned the technological and conceptual domains.

Our third and final research stream consisted of a technique called verbal protocol analysis, which was employed to study performance tasks centered on a societal "grand challenge." We asked 28 leading innovation consultants, innovation executives, university professors, and students viewed as leading innovators to state their thought process as they approached the performance task. The observations were transcribed for analysis and studied to understand and codify patterns of thought and action associated with high-impact innovation pursuits.

The iterative triangulation of these research streams resulted in what we describe as "the enabling innovation model" and a related set of competencies and proactive design behaviors to design for high-impact innovation.[4] This research was conducted with generous support from the Purdue University Engineer of 2020 Initiative, the Consejo Nacional de Ciencia y Tecnologia (CONACYT) from the government of Mexico, and Purdue's Bilsland Strategic Initiatives Fellowship.

Framing Innovation from a New Perspective

Academics have been exploring different aspects of innovation and technological change for several decades.[5] During this period, numerous definitions and classifications have emerged. Our definition characterizes innovation as a "new or different idea introduced into use or practice that has a positive impact on society."[6] Implicit in this definition are four perspectives that embrace and extend beyond historical frameworks and inform proactive innovation design and development: the perspectives of solutions, users, problems, and impact.[7]

Traditionally, researchers focused on characterizing innovation from a solution perspective (for instance, radical, incremental, product, and process innovation, or general purpose technology).[8] Subsequent work highlighted the benefit of taking a user perspective and called attention to the importance of addressing a latent need or problem (for example, disruptive or market-creating innovations that address "jobs to be done").[9] However, innovation impact—the driver of adoption and subsequent economic success—has historically been overlooked except in retrospective assessments of economic metrics such as job creation, productivity gains, and capital returns.

The potential to achieve impact can guide decisions that managers must make to screen, shape, and develop innovations. Rather than thinking about impact retrospectively, we can, in fact, think about impact proactively. To appreciate how impact works, we developed an innovation impact model that looks at impact along four dimensions: reach, significance, paradigm change, and longevity:[10]

- *Reach* measures the breadth of influence and refers to the number of individuals, groups, and societal segments affected by an innovation.
- *Significance* refers to the magnitude of benefits across measures of economics, environment, health, and culture driven by an innovation.

- *Paradigm change* conveys the degree to which an innovation changes implicit or explicit worldviews in a particular domain.

- *Longevity* speaks to how long an innovation is able to exert influence.

Examining impact from these perspectives can help both business leaders and policymakers understand how innovations drive large-scale change in people's lives. For example, Apple Inc.'s efforts to drive global use of smartphones resulted in changes in lifestyle and social habits, expansion of economic value chains and ecosystems, and installation of new infrastructure to drive increased connectivity. Similarly, getting 1 billion people to join Facebook required far-reaching changes in how people communicate and manage personal relationships.

Compared with other types of innovation, enabling innovations excel in each of the impact dimensions we have named.[11] They can satisfy multiple purposes across contexts, which in turn gives them the ability to deliver exceptional impact. In exploring how enabling innovations work, the focus isn't just on users, their problems, or related solutions—though these perspectives are important—but also on how the impact unfolds and the strategies that can be used to proactively shape it.

A Model of Innovation Impact

In evaluating innovations by their impact, we have found that there are three major stages that occur over time: *the breakthrough period, the enabling window,* and what we refer to as *the progressive innovation cascade.*[12]

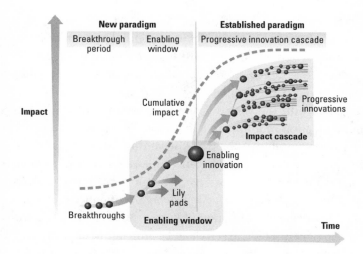

The Enabling Innovation Model

Enabling innovations form the foundation for a cascade of *progressive innovations* that serve a broad array of purposes in multiple contexts and drive a change in paradigm, collectively driving tremendous cumulative impact. These innovations can typically be traced back to a series of fundamental breakthroughs. Between the *breakthrough* period and the impact cascade there is a critical stage called the *enabling window*. Decisions made in the enabling window (including decisions to string together a series of *lily pad* markets) allow organizations to build capabilities and explore markets that affect the timing and magnitude of impact achieved.

The Breakthrough Period

Driving the significant impact that stems from an enabling innovation typically begins with breakthroughs: technical discoveries, inventions, or conceptual leaps that represent a step change even if they initially have little impact. That is what happened with the Global Positioning System (GPS), which is the foundation of a host of applications including automobile navigation systems, Google Maps, and an array of handheld and wearable devices. GPS began with a series of breakthrough insights more than 50 years ago, when Johns Hopkins University physicists William Guier and George Weiffenbach invented a way to calculate the location of Russia's Sputnik satellite using its radio signals, a radio receiver, and a principle in physics called the Doppler effect.[13] In the course of their work, Guier and Weiffenbach realized that they could solve the reverse problem as well—that is, calculate the location of a receiver on the ground using the satellite's signals. This discovery led to multiple technical breakthroughs in satellite orbital tracking computations and electromagnetic signal processing to track objects on earth.

Not every enabling innovation begins with technical breakthroughs, however. The development of modern microfinance, for example, was founded largely on conceptual breakthroughs. Muhammad Yunus, founder of the Grameen Bank, conducted observational studies in Bangladesh and studied government and social science definitions of "poor" to develop a deeper understanding of poverty. He understood that mixing people at different tiers of poverty in development programs tended to create disadvantages for the poorest group. A vicious cycle would emerge in which the relatively wealthy would lend the poor capital at interest rates they couldn't afford. Eventually he realized that this cycle could be broken by creating mechanisms to provide microloans.[14]

The Enabling Window

Breakthrough insights by themselves are not enough to drive an idea toward broad, enabling impact. Innovators must navigate the enabling window, the critical stage in which multiple insights and capabilities coalesce. During this stage, innovation leaders often have opportunities to make decisions about which capabilities to develop and which application contexts to pursue that will affect the significance as well as the adoption rate of the innovation.

Through our research, we have found that there are two distinct paths for navigating the enabling window and achieving high impact: the moonshot approach, in which innovators relentlessly stay on one track in a make-or-break effort to accomplish their objective, and the less risky lily pad strategy.

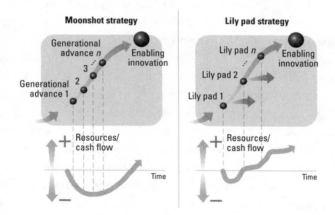

Two Approaches to Navigating the Enabling Window

"Moonshot" innovation initiatives typically involve long periods of significant resource investment in the pursuit of advances in a single application space until the goal is achieved. With "lily pad" strategies, capabilities are developed and introduced opportunistically in application spaces that are ready for adoption. Progress on one lily pad garners resources/cash flow earlier in the development process and can create a pathway for subsequent lily pads in other application spaces.

With the moonshot strategy, an organization pursues the enabling innovation vision relentlessly through small tests and incremental advances in a single, focused application space for as long as it takes to succeed. This often requires significant early commitments of capital and steadfast support. When the objectives are achieved, the benefits can be substantial and can trickle down to other applications. However, because innovations pursued in this way are locked into a vision for a specific application context or collection of capabilities, opportunities to accelerate capability development and realize impact in alternate contexts during the enabling window are mostly ignored. Many times, moonshot efforts fail as financial and political support erodes due to the lack of results, making it difficult to turn breakthroughs into enabling innovations.[15]

With the lily pad strategy, innovators can be more strategic about how they implement their vision. Rather than risking large amounts of resources on one path, they pursue a series of lower-risk initiatives. To do this, they must link the current capabilities of their solutions, whether in parts or as a whole, to end-user needs in application spaces ready to accept them. The goal isn't to satisfy a *specific end user or application* (although innovators typically do have a long-term target end user or application in mind). Rather, it's to satisfy *any end user who will adopt now*.

The reason is simple: Adoption leads to resources and/or cash flow, which allows the work to continue and creates a lily pad upon which the innovation initiative can "land" on its way to a larger goal. The idea is to jump across lily pads—even in spaces that may seem of secondary strategic importance—as early as possible as a means of building interest in the concept (internally and externally), thus retaining the "right" to stay in business, with the eventual goal of bringing together parts of an enabling innovation over time.

For example, consider the differences between how radar technology and mobile robotics were developed. Radar was developed using a classic moonshot strategy. During World War II, researchers across multiple nations worked to develop radar for high-performance military applications, building on earlier breakthroughs. Then, after the war, radar technology "trickled down" into broader applications. By contrast, mobile robotics has followed a course that's consistent with a lily pad strategy. For example, management of iRobot Corp., one of the market leaders, has systematically matched its achievable performance to application contexts that could generate financial returns comparatively rapidly while building awareness and societal acceptance of the underlying technology. iRobot has advanced quickly from breakthroughs from military and space research to applications in oil exploration and extraction, disaster management, and children's toys, to household vacuuming, pool cleaning, maritime applications, and environmental monitoring.

Other examples of enabling innovations have tended to follow a lily pad process as well, albeit unintentionally. Although X-ray technology was originally imagined for medical purposes, early X-ray devices were used for entertainment in department stores and for security and customs inspection in train stations. Dentists were the first to routinely use X-rays in the medical professions: Initially, X-ray devices were better suited to scan teeth than other parts of the body due to exposure time and resolution constraints.[16] These examples illustrate how enabling innovations jump across lily pads while in the enabling window, suggesting that the lily pad strategy can be employed proactively.

The Progressive Innovation Cascade

Innovations transition out of the enabling window and become true enabling innovations once their capabilities are agglomerated and applied in the form of progressive innovations that fulfill different purposes across different contexts. At this point, the innovation can drive a cascade of impacts across multiple dimensions. The laser provides a good example. Lasers changed our ability to ablate material, to measure distance, and to communicate. Not only have lasers spawned new companies, revolutionized medical procedures, and created jobs; the technology, which was developed more than 50 years ago, continues to generate advances today. Conceptual enablers can be just as powerful. The concept of crowdsourcing, for example, has enabled other conceptual innovations, including crowdfunding, citizen science, and the sharing economy, each applying crowdsourcing techniques for different purposes (such as problem solving, pooling resources, curating collections, or identifying patterns), resulting in significant impact.

Because the impact of historical enabling innovations seems obvious in hindsight, the question arises: *How do you proactively spot and shape enabling innovations?*[17] Our research was designed to answer this question. We focused on the identification of proactive patterns of thought and action to make enabling innovation possible.

Spotting Enabling Innovations

A common set of characteristics underpins enabling innovations and makes it possible to spot and shape them. These characteristics can guide leaders in managing their investments in innovation.

Enabling innovations tend to offer multiple pathways from first principles to impact. In essence, a first principles pathway indicates what an innovation can "do" in the most fundamental sense, without ties to a particular industry, application, or context. For example, lasers, at the most fundamental level, are sources of coherent light created through a physics principle called stimulated emission. For its part, crowdsourcing is a mechanism to aggregate resources, which could be insights, money, or emotional support. For any given innovation, thinking about the paths to impact from first principles provides an indication of the innovation's potential and highlights the spectrum of possibilities for achieving impact.

They have relevance to multiple purpose categories. Enabling innovations can be employed in multiple *purpose categories* to solve fundamentally different types of problems. Different purpose categories can be identified by describing the challenges that an enabling innovation can address through a first principles pathway without tying them to a specific context. Coherent light from lasers, for example, can be used for various purposes: to transmit data, ablate material, or measure distance. GPS is widely used for locating objects or people in physical spaces, but it can also be used to measure travel speed or to synchronize timing instruments.

They have utility across many application spaces. Enabling innovations are useful in many application spaces. Crowdsourcing, for instance, is useful when pooling financial resources in a philanthropic context (for example, Kiva) and also in an entrepreneurial context (for instance, Kickstarter). Similarly, radar can be used to detect and avoid objects in navigation and is also

helpful in identifying patterns in geologic formations or meteo-
rology, or in assessing the speed of an approaching vehicle in law
enforcement.

**They offer the potential to change existing societal perspec-
tives.** Enabling innovations expose and/or challenge what we
call *hidden worldviews* to establish new paradigms, reframe familiar problems, or introduce new cultural norms. The history of
anesthesia offers a good example. Before the development of
modern anesthesia, people had a very different notion about
invasive surgery. However, once medical practitioners learned
how to administer anesthesia to manage pain, the criteria for
surgical skill changed—from being fast to being cautious and
accurate.[18]

They offer possibilities for reconfiguring ecosystems. Enabling
innovations often *reconfigure ecosystems*. Take the development
of radar. As radar gained popularity, a network of special anten-
nas was required for applications such as weather prediction,
leading to the emergence of new technology, suppliers, and jobs,
as well as new information that was useful on a daily basis for
consumers and that dramatically affected quality of life. If innovation leaders proactively identify the ecosystem changes that
may stem from an innovation, they can get a sense of the innovation's significance and its potential to be enabling.

They tend to have significant potential for improvement.
Enabling innovations exhibit room for improvement (what we
call *headroom*) to fulfill different purposes or extend to new contexts. The improvements could involve technology, economics,
or ecosystem alignment. For example, early GPS receivers could

receive signals only every few hours, which limited the potential applications. Early X-ray devices had similar constraints; they took several hours to generate images. However, the potential for improvements can often be envisioned early. Innovation roadmaps founded on what-if analyses can highlight priority capabilities, preview new application spaces, and suggest possible alternate development paths.

They offer diverse solution forms and combinations. Enabling innovations can manifest in an array of solution forms and combinations. Radar, for example, comes in multiple forms. It can be pulsed or continuous, active or passive, unidirectional or bidirectional, or Doppler. The same goes for lasers, which can be based on various substances, including gas, liquid chemicals, solid-state gain media, or semiconductors. The versatility of enabling innovations can be enhanced when used in combination with other innovations.

They drive a foreseeable impact cascade. Enabling innovations generate a *foreseeable impact cascade*. As a result, leaders and decision makers can identify enablers by projecting the reach, significance, paradigm change, and longevity potential of innovations. For example, manipulating the X-ray region in the electromagnetic spectrum, although often associated with monitoring and improving people's health, also stimulated the creation of new industries (for example, protective clothing and exposure sensors), provided new ways to scan our environment (such as X-ray astronomy), and shaped many elements of culture (for instance, improved security through luggage inspection). Frequently, many of the benefits are apparent long before they are implemented.

Realizing Enabling Innovations

Once an organization understands the characteristics of enabling innovations, what can management do to create and capture them? Based on our research, we have identified four enabling actions:

Screen for the characteristics of enabling innovations at the front end. All ideas (or components of ideas) should be screened based on the characteristics described above. Such screening can help decision makers understand whether their investments and the path to development should be considered as an enabling innovation or a progressive innovation, or whether there's a specific component of the innovation that could be further developed. GPS provides a good example. Early in its development, those in the field recognized its potential to be applied for many purposes in multiple contexts, and they even began to articulate some of the important issues that needed to be addressed (such as security and privacy).[19] Not only has the underlying technology of GPS been applied across many different contexts, but it continues to provide solutions that have far-reaching implications for society.

Envision and proactively pursue lily pad markets to fuel the development of desired capabilities. Lily pad applications for an enabling innovation provide opportunities to match capability, purpose, and context in a manner that advances select performance dimensions of the innovation, aligns elements of ecosystems, and/or begins to shift worldviews. Many high-impact innovations have unfolded this way. For example, a series of

A "lily pad" strategy can generate critical resources needed for continued development of a concept, reducing the time to results and reducing the overall level of risk.

capability-building lily pads related to the uses and production of glass are at the foundation of fiber optics.

One of the very first applications of light-guiding glass was to illuminate teeth for dental exams.[20] Later, optical fibers were used in medical settings for remote illumination and in the military to enhance visual range. Improvements in glass production and expanded transmission bands opened up other applications, such as fiber-optic long-distance communication. A similar proliferation of capabilities has taken place in mobile robotics.[21] Feedback from early applications can be used to identify future development paths that lead to other potential lily pads.

Monetize steps along the way by going beyond common industry boundaries. Beyond solution optimization, a lily pad strategy can generate critical resources needed for continued development of a concept, reducing the time to results and reducing the overall level of risk. The key is to be proactive and expansive in defining new application spaces. Many managers are reluctant to apply ideas beyond the context in which they were conceived. However, this view ignores the possibilities for faster adoption of solutions in other contexts. The development of silicon transistors offers a good example of how monetization forms can vary along lily pads.

Although Bell Labs pioneered the germanium transistor, it was Texas Instruments Inc. (TI), originally a Dallas-based company providing seismic exploration services to the oil industry, that played the pivotal role in advancing the enabling innovation. While TI had a license to manufacture transistors from Bell Labs, it saw more potential in developing silicon transistors than in germanium transistors, which if successful would be cheaper to make. To monetize its investments, TI employed a strategy that resembled a lily pad approach. First, it partnered with another company to make transistors for pocket radios; then it developed some of the first commercially available microchips, which were sold to the military and the space program.[22] TI's next—and most dramatic—leap was into high-volume pocket calculators for consumers. Similarly, the early history of synthetic chemistry, although originally intended for human health purposes, can be traced back to the synthetic dye industry. Many Swiss and German companies, such as Bayer AG, monetized chemical capabilities in dyes before becoming pharmaceutical companies.[23]

The proactive pursuit of lily pad application spaces requires going beyond the usual strategic boundaries. This may require monetizing developments via a different business model, or making trade-offs that might not be viewed as optimal using traditional lenses. Before launching the Roomba vacuum, for example, iRobot explored multiple monetization paths. As the first step, it garnered research contracts with the military and space exploration agencies. Then it pursued commercial partnerships with S. C. Johnson & Son, the cleaning supply company, and Hasbro Inc., the toy company. Each of these lily pads provided a distinct insight into the technology and how it could be monetized, without causing the innovator (in this case, iRobot) to lose sight of the longer-term goal of a broader enabling innovation.

Understand and proactively shape the ecosystem. Organizations that wish to achieve enabling innovations must be ready to articulate, structure, and proactively address the broad spectrum of forces at work in the ecosystems that the innovator may encounter throughout the enabling window. These forces span the systemic, technical, economic, sociological, and psychological domains; they can include traditional factors such as the presence of alternative solutions and regulations, as well as less commonly examined issues such as prevailing norms and deeply seated paradigms that could limit change.

Prior to the rise of anesthesia, for example, surgical skill was measured in terms of speed; even in the early days after its introduction, many people considered anesthesia a "needless luxury."[24] Years of live surgical exhibitions, academic publications, and patient testimonials were required to shift the surgical community's practices. Life insurance faced similar cultural resistance from people who objected to placing a monetary value on life and death. Today, innovative organizations are demonstrating an awareness of broader ecosystem issues and driving the change they need to realize their vision. For example, Google Inc. designs its own servers optimized for data center efficiency, and Amazon.com Inc. leases fleets of cargo planes to address its massive demand for freight transportation.

The net result of these philosophies is that enabling innovations can develop more quickly, with increased opportunities for self-funding and reduced levels of risk. With the lily pad approach, organizations may not work with their ideal end users or in their preferred contexts at the outset. Nevertheless, their activities may advance them toward their long-term goal. In the case of iRobot, although the company wanted to use robots to solve problems that affected people's lives, to generate the revenue it needed it maintained flexibility by developing products and capabilities in several new arenas that were outside its target market.[25] By doing so, it broadened its expertise. The company continues to pursue this strategy, adapting its capabilities and business model to such new markets as law enforcement, homeland security, elder care, home automation, landscaping, agriculture, and construction.[26] In this respect, iRobot has strategically understood its capabilities and pathways to impact from a first principles perspective and made connections to lily pads that have allowed the company to advance.

While we acknowledge that some efforts to innovate are binary (they either succeed or they don't, and it often takes time and effort to find out), many are not. What's more, even environments that seem suited to moonshots lend themselves to identifying opportunities for lily pads, as the capabilities needed to develop enabling innovations in these types of environments are likely to be relevant in other domains. For example, back in the 1880s, Pfizer Inc.'s research into fermentation led to chemical advances in the production of citric acid that had applications in the manufacture of soft drinks such as Coca-Cola and Pepsi, which were growing in popularity at the end of the 19th century. Not only did these capabilities provide the company with decades of growth; they helped the pharmaceutical company develop deep-tank fermentation methods later used for the production of penicillin.[27] Indeed, it's possible that advances can be achieved that generate significant value—either scientifically or from a market perspective—if applied to other settings immediately.

Getting Ready for Enabling Innovations

By successfully spotting, shaping, and pursuing enabling innovations using lily pad strategies, organizations can reduce the risk of pursuing high-impact opportunities that can drive enduring growth. We recognize, however, that proactive use of the approaches and insights outlined here is nontrivial, and it likely requires leaders to carefully rethink many elements of their approach to innovation. To improve their ability to innovate effectively, organizations can benefit by considering the following questions:

Do you understand the role of enabling innovation in your strategy? Although we focus heavily on enabling innovation in this chapter, other forms of innovation can (and should) be part of a balanced innovation portfolio. Achieving the right timing and balance for enabling innovation in your organization's innovation portfolio requires understanding the organization's history and having a view on its future environment. Many organizations are operating right now on the cascade created by a previous enabling innovation, and when that enabling innovation runs its course, such organizations will need to find another one. Understanding where your organization is in the enabling innovation model can help inform your strategy and determine how much effort you should dedicate to spotting and capturing an enabling innovation.

Can you spot potential enabling innovations? Employing the insights described here may require innovation teams to think differently. By asking who might want to use this capability, organizations are opening up new paths, at least some of which are counterintuitive and uncertain. However, engaging in this exercise can help would-be innovators appreciate their possibilities and prioritize potential investments using a powerful lens.

Do you have the business model flexibility to pursue a lily pad strategy? Succeeding with enabling innovation requires an organization to have the business model flexibility to monetize lily pad applications. This can be done in many ways, such as developing a strong licensing capability for your intellectual property; experimenting with partnerships, alliances, and consortia; or diversifying your business entirely. To fully take advantage of lily pad opportunities while running your core business, you may need to become comfortable identifying and pursuing new business models.[28]

Do you have the organizational will to pursue enabling innovations? True enabling innovations can yield rewards that go far beyond most other forms of innovation and give companies a long-lasting competitive edge. However, pursuing them may seem at odds with the pressure for short-term results. To be sure, challenging the norms of your current business environment to explore new lily pad markets will not be easy. But our approach offers an opportunity for organizations to invest both for now and for the future.

In an increasingly unpredictable and resource-constrained world, accelerated, lower-risk pursuit of enabling innovations could be a key to long-term success. Such innovations offer the potential to create enduring growth for the organizations driving them, not simply based on their functional or conceptual advances, but also because of the influence they can have on broader societal factors that can drive widespread adoption and use across multiple application spaces. It is their ability to change society that drives economic gains, not the other way around. Managers would do well to be aware of this counterintuitive cause–effect relationship in advance. In matters of innovation, risk, and return, understanding enabling innovations and lily pad strategies can lead executives to smarter (and less risky) decision-making and investment strategies.

Notes

1. The classical risk–return doctrine has its origins in microeconomics, portfolio theory, and capital allocation models, with the capital asset pricing model being a prime example. This model states that the expected risk premium of an investment is proportional to its (undiversifiable) systemic risk, meaning that increased risk should be rewarded with commensurately higher returns.

2. See V. Bush, *Science: The Endless Frontier* (Washington, DC: US Government Printing Office, 1945); D. E. Stokes, *Pasteur's Quadrant: Basic Science and Technological Innovation* (Washington, DC: Brookings Institution Press, 1997); and J. M. Dudley, "Defending Basic Research," *Nature Photonics* 7, no. 5 (2013): 338–339.

3. See F. G. Solis, "Characterizing Enabling Innovations and Enabling Thinking" (PhD dissertation, Purdue University, School of Civil Engineering, 2015); F. Solis and J. Sinfield, "Rethinking Innovation: Characterizing Dimensions of Impact" (paper presented at the ASEE Annual Conference and Exposition: 360 Degrees of Engineering Education, Indianapolis, Indiana, June 15–18, 2014); and F. Solis and J. V. Sinfield, "Rethinking Innovation: Characterizing Dimensions of Impact," *Journal of Engineering Entrepreneurship* 6, no. 2 (2015): 83–96.

4. Solis, "Characterizing Enabling Innovations."

5. See B. Godin, "Innovation Studies: The Invention of a Specialty (Part I)," (Montreal, Quebec: Project on the Intellectual History of Innovation, working paper 7, 2010); and B. Godin, "Innovation Studies: The Invention of a Specialty (Part II)," (Montreal, Quebec: Project on the Intellectual History of Innovation, working paper 8, 2010).

6. Solis and Sinfield, "Rethinking Innovation," 83.

7. Solis and Sinfield, 83.

8. Until relatively recently, most definitions of innovation were focused on solutions—in particular, technical solutions. Solutions were characterized by their novelty and the way they differed from prior solutions. Product and process innovations focused on improvements to what was already available. Solutions that have broad applicability (such as the steam engine, electrification, and the internet) have often been called

general purpose technologies, or GPTs. Beginning in the 1990s, researchers also began paying close attention to service innovations and business model innovations. These involve changes in how solutions are designed and implemented, but they don't always involve new technology. See J. M. Utterback and W. J. Abernathy, "A Dynamic Model of Process and Product Innovation," *Omega, The International Journal of Management Science* 3, no. 6 (1975): 639–656; J. E. Ettlie, W. P. Bridges, and R. D. O'Keefe, "Organization Strategy and Structural Differences For Radical Versus Incremental Innovation," *Management Science* 30, no. 6 (1984): 682–695; and T. F. Bresnahan and M. Trajtenberg, "General Purpose Technologies 'Engines of Growth?'" *Journal of Econometrics* 65, no. 1 (1995): 83–108.

9. Also in the 1990s, a new perspective on innovation began to focus on end users. Rather than looking at developments in comparison to prior solutions, researchers examined what users found important. In his work on disruptive innovation, Harvard Business School professor Clayton M. Christensen found that some users were willing to make significant trade-offs in performance and forgo traditional benefits based on what they sought to accomplish in their own circumstances, particularly when they were constrained by wealth, time, access, or expertise. An extension of this work has focused on market-creating innovations, as exemplified by Ford Motor Co.'s Model T and the personal computer. Such innovations democratize complicated or costly products for markets that previously didn't exist. See C. M. Christensen, *The Innovator's Dilemma: When New Technologies Cause Great Firms to Fail* (Boston, MA: Harvard Business Press, 1997); C. M. Christensen and D. van Bever, "The Capitalist's Dilemma," *Harvard Business Review* 92, no. 6 (2014): 60–68; and S. D. Anthony, M. W. Johnson, J. V. Sinfield, and E. J. Altman, *The Innovator's Guide to Growth: Putting Disruptive Innovation to Work* (Boston, MA: Harvard Business Press, 2008).

10. Solis and Sinfield, "Rethinking Innovation": 88–89.

11. Solis and Sinfield, 88–89; and Solis, "Characterizing Enabling Innovations."

12. Our research suggests that this pattern is equally applicable to large-scale socioeconomic and systems-level challenges often encountered in nonprofit and government contexts.

13. See H. Bray, *You Are Here: From the Compass to GPS, the History and Future of How We Find Ourselves* (New York: Basic Books, 2014); and W. H. Guier and G. C. Weiffenbach, "Genesis of Satellite Navigation," *Johns Hopkins Technical Digest* 19, no. 1 (1998): 14–17.

14. M. Yunus, *Banker to the Poor: Micro-Lending and the Battle against World Poverty* (New York: Public Affairs, 1999).

15. See D. Dougherty and C. Hardy, "Sustained Product Innovation in Large, Mature Organizations: Overcoming Innovation-to-Organization Problems," *Academy of Management Journal* 39, no. 5 (1996): 1120–1153; E. Maine and E. Garnsey, "Commercializing Generic Technology: The Case of Advanced Materials Ventures," *Research Policy* 35, no. 3 (2006): 375–393; N. Matta and R. Ashkenas, "Why Good Projects Fail Anyway," *Harvard Business Review* 81, no. 9 (2003): 109–116; B. J. Sauser, R. R. Reilly, and A. J. Shenhar, "Why Projects Fail? How Contingency Theory Can Provide New Insights—A Comparative Analysis of NASA's Mars Climate Orbiter Loss," *International Journal of Project Management* 27, no. 7 (2009): 665–679; and L. R. Cohen and R. G. Noll, "Government R&D Programs for Commercializing Space," *American Economic Review* 76, no. 2 (1986): 269–273.

16. See B. H. Kevles, *Naked to the Bone: Medical Imaging in the Twentieth Century* (New Brunswick, NJ: Rutgers University Press, 1997); and R. B. Gunderman, *X-Ray Vision: The Evolution of Medical Imaging and Its Human Significance* (New York: Oxford University Press, 2012).

17. In fact, the enabling-progressive pattern suggests that a handful of solutions underpin a tremendous amount of impact that can be exploited by businesses, agencies, foundations, and societies alike.

18. See A. Gawande, "Two Hundred Years of Surgery," *New England Journal of Medicine* 366, no. 18 (2012): 1716–1723; and A. Gawande, "Slow Ideas," *New Yorker*, July 29, 2013, https://www.newyorker.com/magazine/2013/07/29/slow-ideas.

19. Bray, "You Are Here."

20. J. Hecht, *City of Light: The Story of Fiber Optics* (New York: Oxford University Press, 2004).

21. In what could be considered lily pads to mobile robotics, iRobot developed capabilities in spatial exploration through the Genghis robot, in real-time data gathering through MicroRig, in real-time interactions

through the toy My Real Baby and the robot IT, in navigation and mobility through the Gecko and Holon robots, and in floor cleaning through the NexGen Floor Care Solution. See iRobot, "Cool Stuff: The Story of Our Robots," https://www.irobot.com/filelibrary/ppt/corp/cool_stuff_ppt/cool_stuff_ppt.html.

22. W. Isaacson, *The Innovators: How a Group of Hackers, Geniuses, and Geeks Created the Digital Revolution* (New York: Simon & Schuster, 2014).

23. For example, while attempting to synthesize an antimalarial agent, two scientists unexpectedly produced a purple compound that turned out to be a synthetic dye. Recognizing the potential to exploit this synthetic chemistry capability, many Swiss and German companies, including IG Farben (part of which was later split off as Bayer), led the creation of the synthetic dye industry. Eventually, the capabilities developed by these companies in the manufacture of synthetic dyes helped them transform into modern pharmaceutical companies and led to important successes in human health applications such as aspirin, antibacterials, and chemotherapy. See B. J. Yeh and W. A. Lim, "Synthetic Biology: Lessons from the History of Synthetic Organic Chemistry," *Nature Chemical Biology* 3, no. 9 (2007): 521–525.

24. Gawande, "Two Hundred Years"; and Gawande, "Slow Ideas."

25. iRobot, "2014 Annual Report," http://investor.irobot.com/financial-information/annual-reports.

26. iRobot, "2014 Annual Report."

27. J. Ginsberg, *Development of Deep-Tank Fermentation, Pfizer Inc.* (Washington, DC: American Chemical Society, 2008).

28. J. V. Sinfield, E. Calder, B. McConnell, and S. Colson, "How to Identify New Business Models," *MIT Sloan Management Review* 53, no. 2 (2012): 85–90.

6

The Flare and Focus of Successful Futurists

Amy Webb

Futurists are skilled at listening to and interpreting signals, which are harbingers of what's to come. They look for early patterns—pretrends, if you will—as the scattered points on the fringe converge and begin moving toward the mainstream. The fringe is that place where hackers are experimenting, academics are testing their ideas, technologists are building new prototypes, and so on. Futurists know most patterns will come to nothing, so they watch and wait and test the patterns to find those few that will evolve into genuine trends. Each trend is a looking glass into the future, a way to see over time's horizon. This is the art of forecasting the future: simultaneously recognizing patterns in the present and thinking about how those changes will impact the future so that you can be actively engaged in building what happens next—or at least be less surprised by what others develop. Futures forecasting is a learnable skill, and a process any organization can master.

Joseph Voros, a theoretical physicist and senior lecturer in strategic foresight at Swinburne University of Technology in Melbourne, Australia, offers my favorite explanation of futures forecasting, saying it informs strategy making by enhancing the "context within which strategy is developed, planned, and executed."[1] The advantage of forecasting the future in this way is obvious: Organizations that can see trends early can better prepare to take advantage of them. They can also help shape the broader context, with an understanding of how developments in seemingly unconnected industries will affect them. Most organizations that track emerging trends are adept at conversing and collaborating with those in other fields to plan ahead.

Although futures studies is an established academic discipline, few companies employ futurists. That's starting to change as more leaders become familiar with the work futurists do. Accenture, Ford, Google, IBM, Intel, Samsung, and UNESCO all have had futurists on staff, and their work is quite different from what happens within the traditional research and development (R&D) function.

The futurists at these organizations know that their tools are best used within a group—and that the group's composition matters tremendously to the outcomes they produce. Here's why. Within every organization are people whose dominant characteristic is either creativity or logic. If you've been on a team that included both groups and didn't have a great facilitator during your meetings, your team probably clashed. If it was an important project and there were strong personalities representing each side, the creative people felt as though their contributions were being discounted, while the logical thinkers—whose natural talents lie in managing processes, projecting budgets, or mitigating risk—felt undervalued because they weren't coming up with bold new ideas. Your team undoubtedly had a difficult time staying on track, or worse, you might have spent hours meeting about how to have your next meeting. I call this the "duality dilemma."

The duality dilemma is responsible for a lack of forward thinking at many organizations. It contributed to the decline of BlackBerry Ltd.'s smartphone business; the company (formerly known as Research in Motion Ltd.) never had an executable plan to remake the phone's form factor and operating system in the age of the iPhone. Right-brained creatives wanted to make serious changes to the phone, while left-brained process thinkers were fixated on risk and maintaining BlackBerry's customer base.[2] The future of the business hinged on the company's ability to bring both forces together to forecast trends and plan for the future.

BlackBerry's experience suggests that forecasting the future of a product, company, or industry should neither be relegated to inventive visionaries nor mapped entirely by left-brain thinkers. Futures forecasting is meant to unite opposing forces, harnessing both wild imagination and pragmatism.

Turning a Dilemma into a Dynamic

Overcoming the duality dilemma—and getting full use of both your creative- and logic-oriented team members—in order to track emerging trends and forecast the future is possible. But counterintuitively, it's a matter of highlighting—rather than discouraging or downplaying—the strengths of each side. Stanford University's Hasso Plattner Institute of Design (also known as the d.school) teaches a brainstorming technique that addresses the duality dilemma and illuminates how an organization can harness both strengths in equal measure by alternately broadening ("flaring") and narrowing ("focusing") its thinking.[3]

When a team is flaring, it is finding inspiration, making lists of ideas, mapping out new possibilities, getting feedback, and

thinking big. When it is focusing, those ideas must be investi-
gated, vetted, and decided upon. Flaring asks questions such as:
What if? Who could it be? Why might this matter? What might
be the implications of our actions? Focusing asks: Which option
is best? What is our next action? How do we move forward?

The forecasting method I have developed—one, of course,
influenced by other futurists but different in analysis and
scope—is a six-step process that I have refined during the past
decade as part of my work at the Future Today Institute. The
first four steps involve finding a trend, while the last two steps
inform what action you should then take.

The dynamic of flare and focus is woven through this forecasting methodology. The six steps require teams to alternate
between flaring and focusing, harnessing the dominant qualities
of the right brain and the left brain. With each step, you are able
to understand the likely future of the topic you're examining
more clearly as you define a trend, determine the best action to
take, and create and test your strategy. When you both flare and
focus, you are able to overcome the duality dilemma.

Here's how to use these complementary ways of thinking:

First, flare at the fringe. Keep an open mind as you cast a wide
enough net and gather information without judgment. This
involves creating a map of what you observe at the fringe. This
map should show nodes—or key concepts, companies, places,
and people—and the relationships between them. Think of it as
rounding up the "unusual suspects." You're brainstorming, making a fringe map, forcing yourself to think outside the box and
consider radically different points of view.

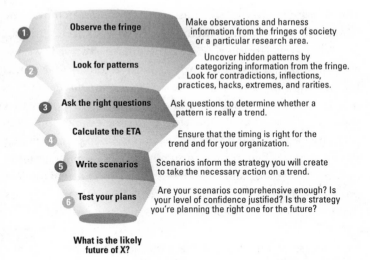

1. **Observe the fringe** — Make observations and harness information from the fringes of society or a particular research area.

2. **Look for patterns** — Uncover hidden patterns by categorizing information from the fringe. Look for contradictions, inflections, practices, hacks, extremes, and rarities.

3. **Ask the right questions** — Ask questions to determine whether a pattern is really a trend.

4. **Calculate the ETA** — Ensure that the timing is right for the trend and for your organization.

5. **Write scenarios** — Scenarios inform the strategy you will create to take the necessary action on a trend.

6. **Test your plans** — Are your scenarios comprehensive enough? Is your level of confidence justified? Is the strategy you're planning the right one for the future?

What is the likely future of X?

A Six-Step Forecasting Methodology

The six steps in this forecasting methodology require teams to alternate between broadening (that is, "flaring") and narrowing (that is, "focusing") their thinking.

Focus to spot patterns. You must narrow your research from the fringe and uncover the patterns hidden in your sketch to spot possible trends. To categorize what we have observed, we use a framework called CIPHER, which is an acronym that stands for *contradictions, inflections, practices, hacks, extremes*, and *rarities*. Look for surprising contradictions; inflection points that signal an acceleration of some change in progress; new practices that upset established norms (for example, when people altered the long-established norm of watching television programming only on TVs); hacks and adjustments that users are making to a product or technology to make it work better for them; extremes that push boundaries to break new ground; and rarities.[4]

Flare to ask the right questions. Determine whether a pattern really is a trend or merely a trendy flash in the pan. You will be tempted to stop looking once you've spotted a pattern; most forecasters never force themselves to poke holes into every single assumption and assertion they make. But you will soon learn that creating counterarguments is an essential part of the forecasting process.

Focus to calculate timing. Interpret the trend, and ensure that the timing is right. This isn't just about finding the typical S-curve that managers rely on to describe adoptions of a new innovation or technology; such an S-curve can show a new technology's adoption, but it does not offer a full picture of how external effects (such as a change in government leadership or a natural disaster) could affect its development. As technology trends move along their trajectories, two forces are in play—internal developments within tech companies, and external developments within the government, adjacent businesses, and the like—and both must be considered.

Flare to create scenarios and strategies. First, build scenarios to create probable, plausible, and possible futures; then create strategies to accompany them. Probable scenarios represent the most likely outcomes if there are no unexpected major changes in circumstances, while plausible scenarios allow for many facets of daily life—some that we might not be able to imagine now—to change dramatically. Meanwhile, possible scenarios assume that nothing is set in stone—and that life as we know it could look radically different than it does today.

This step requires thinking about both the timeline of a technology's development and your emotional reactions to all the possible outcomes. What necessary strategies and ways of thinking will govern how your organization will respond to the trend? Score each scenario with an estimated likelihood of occurrence and, on the basis of your analysis, create a corresponding strategy for action. A score of less than 40% suggests either you haven't analyzed enough data or it is too early in the timeline to act; a score of more than 70% indicates that you've likely waited too long and should respond quickly.

Focus to test your plans. But what if the action you choose to take in response to a trend is the wrong one? In this final step, you must try to test whether the strategy you create to address a trend will deliver the desired outcome, and that requires asking difficult questions about both the present and the future. These questions should confirm that (1) your organization has confidence in the strategy and will support it; (2) the strategy offers your customers a unique value proposition; (3) you can track the developing trend and measure your outcomes; (4) the strategy communicates a sense of urgency to your staff and to your intended audience; (5) you have the resources needed to

You must try to test whether the strategy you create to address a trend will deliver the desired outcome, and that requires asking difficult questions about both the present and the future.

recalibrate the strategy if and when needed; and (6) the strategy is robust enough to easily accommodate change.

Duality in Action

Any organization intent on surviving and thriving into the future must practice both flaring and focusing in whatever methodology it uses to spot trends, so it is of paramount importance that every team charged with watching and acting on trends include both creative and logical types. Organizations that learn how to balance each hemisphere of the human brain are uniquely positioned to forecast trends and develop strategies that work.

And as you analyze emerging trends, remember: There are never any completely new technologies invented out of whole cloth. Our technology trends, their adoption for use in business, and the cultural, political, educational, and economic shifts that happen concurrently are all interwoven. Our tapestry of invention is part of a continuum over time. The tools may change—from hands, to weavers, to industrial machines, to algorithms and robots, to self-generating synthetic organics—but the previous corpus of research always becomes the basis for fresh thinking at the fringe.

The future is something we are creating now, in the present tense. You have the ability not only to forecast what's to come but also to help create your own preferred future. Don't wait.

Notes

1. J. Voros, "A Primer on Futures Studies, Foresight, and the Use of Scenarios," *Foresight Bulletin*, no. 6 (2001).
2. S. Silcoff, J. McNish, and S. Ladurantaye, "Inside the Fall of Black-Berry: How the Smartphone Inventor Failed to Adapt," *Globe and Mail*, September 27, 2013.

3. See, for example, the d.school's necktie model of flare and focus: T. Winograd, "Design Process Diagrams," n.d., http://hci.stanford.edu/dschool/resources/design-process/gallery.html.

4. For more on these six categories, see A. Webb, "The Tech Trends You Need to Know for 2016," December 8, 2015, https://www.linkedin.com/pulse/tech-trends-you-need-know-2016-amy-webb.

7

Why Design Thinking in Business Needs a Rethink

Martin Kupp, Jamie Anderson, and Jörg Reckhenrich

In recent years, "design thinking" has become popular in many industries as established companies have tried to apply designers' problem-solving techniques to corporate innovation processes.[1] Key elements of the design thinking methodology include fast iterations; early and frequent interaction with customers; agile process design with less hierarchy; and a learning-by-doing approach that involves building prototypes and creating mock-ups of any kind as early as possible in the process.

Here's how design thinking initiatives are supposed to unfold in a corporate setting: A clearly defined innovation challenge is presented to a team trained in design thinking. The team conducts research to better understand the problem. Drawing on its insights, the team proposes a variety of solutions, starts building prototypes, and in the end, identifies a fresh, profitable business opportunity.

That's how the process is supposed to work—but it hardly ever does. Over the past seven years, we have helped more than 20 companies pursue more than 50 design thinking initiatives and have found that such initiatives rarely proceed according to the textbook model. Innovation is an inherently messy process, made even messier because it conflicts in many ways with established processes, structures, and corporate cultures. Fortunately, once you understand the challenges, you can avoid the most common pitfalls.

The root of most of the problems is the disconnect between design thinking and conventional business processes. After all, most companies' successes are built on delivering predictable products by repeatable means. That means organizations almost instinctively resist bringing fuzzy, messy, and abstract vision into the equation. This antipathy toward design thinking runs deep, all the way from the C-suite to line workers. We find that employees often try to dodge design thinking assignments, shying away from the habits and mind-sets the methodology requires.

The organization of the teams themselves leads to a second difficulty. The design thinking methodology calls for egalitarian, self-organized teams, but this isn't how most established large companies work. In fact, the design thinking teams we have studied tend to have clear process and project owners, usually senior managers. These managers not only supervise the design thinking project but also assign tasks to team members and are responsible for its outcome. To make things worse, these senior leaders often supervise 12–15 design thinking projects at a time. This maximizes the leader's time but reduces the teams' efficiency, hinders passion and commitment, and slows progress.

In many companies, four cultural factors tend to aggravate these structural limitations:

Specialization

Specialization often leads to a tacit agreement that makes certain tasks the territory of certain departments. This has two effects on design thinking. First, participants from different departments often have difficulty communicating because of their very specific viewpoints. Second, many people who belong to departments that are traditionally considered less creative, such as accounting or internal audit, suffer from low levels of what management thinkers David and Tom Kelley call "creative confidence."[2] If you've never been encouraged to see innovation as part of your job and have been told that you're no good at it, you'll probably take people's word for it. This may reduce friction and make the organization function more comfortably, but it also reduces the chance of a creative spark.

Human speed bumps

Managers in some departments (particularly legal, compliance, and regulatory affairs) tend to see their role as basically to stop things from happening. To get the most out of a design thinking exercise, people in these departments must embrace a can-do attitude and focus their creative energies on exploring how else things can be done. It takes a special kind of leadership to enable this supportive culture in traditionally conservative and risk-averse functional domains.

A focus on monetary results

In projects with a high degree of novelty, the expectation should be around the amount of learning that takes place, not the result. Focusing too early on monetary results (or other metrics) can discourage creativity—and ironically, reduce the chances of a profitable long-term result.

Failure phobia

Many established companies punish failure, which discourages the risk-taking design thinking requires. In a workshop with a large consumer goods company, we asked participants to formulate hypotheses regarding consumers' buying behavior in one product category. Instead of formulating useful hypotheses, participants developed ones that were so broad and unspecific that they would be impossible to test. We soon realized that the workshop attendees were avoiding mistakes for which they could be held accountable. Unfortunately, reducing their personal risk of failure meant reducing their collective chance of success.

Our research suggests that companies need to take five steps to take full advantage of the potential of design thinking:

Step 1: Encourage top managers to champion design thinking initiatives. We find that design thinking teams require two kinds of attention by top management: proactive and follow-up. Proactive attention comes in many forms, such as launching an initiative, taking part in the process, developing and submitting ideas, and removing obstacles. *Follow-up* attention is the energy the leader invests after the design thinking team does its work, such as pushing ideas through the organization and sometimes giving explicit feedback when ideas are not pursued. Such behaviors can help embed and sustain design thinking in established organizations.

However, the biggest limiting factor is that managers are spread far too thin. Rather than try to monitor the progress of 12 to 15 design thinking initiatives, managers are better off pursuing a single design thinking goal at a time.

Step 2: Balance the teams. Balancing intuitive and analytical thinking is one of the biggest challenges when establishing an innovative culture. Such teams are very tricky for established organizations to manage, as it is difficult to allow people freedom while at the same time ensuring that they don't lose focus on other important business goals.

One key is for team members to recognize and appreciate the diversity of their experience and skills. For example, some members might focus more on workshop facilitation, whereas others may use their personal networks within the company to identify potential projects. The teams should include all pertinent functions, including marketing, sales, product management, and research and development.

Step 3: Set ground rules. Design thinking teams need a lot of autonomy to function well. They should be empowered to act without getting permission for every tiny step. A good way to do this is to set minimal rules for the team, for example, by writing a list of five things they are not allowed to do, such as endanger brand perception or engage in illegal activities. Everything else, by default, they are allowed to do.

Step 4: Integrate design thinking into product-development processes. Design thinking is often treated as yet another assignment from headquarters—just one more box to be checked. To change that perception, the teams responsible for design thinking should look more closely at their existing product-development processes. It can be helpful to integrate specific design thinking deliverables, such as early customer feedback in the problem-definition phase, larger-scale customer feedback in the market-solution phase, and prototypes and mock-ups throughout the process. Linking design thinking to innovation strategy should make it easier to measure the influence of design thinking on the quality and market fit of new products and services. More stakeholders will then see it as an integral part of product development, and not a parallel process.

Step 5: Redefine the metrics. Because design thinking is about the early phase of the innovation process, teams should focus not on profit but on learning. By clearly defining learning outcomes through questions (such as "Why don't patients sign the consent form?"), you can then define precise hypotheses (such as "because the form is too long" or "because the language is incomprehensible"). Even if the overall project fails, the captured learning will lead you to a better question or another project.

Supporting Design Thinking

Too many enterprises have naively invested in training employees in design thinking methodologies, and then been disappointed when they don't see a tangible impact on innovation outcomes. Innovation is an inherently social process that involves not only inventing but also convincing people to do something in a new way. To be successful, a design thinking program must be closely linked with the organization's social dynamics. Without the right supporting mechanisms, you probably won't achieve the desired results.

Notes

1. Peter G. Rowe's book *Design Thinking*, published in 1987, was the first publication to use the term. The book described a systematic approach to problem solving used by architects and urban planners. The application of design thinking methodologies beyond architecture emerged in the 2000s; instrumental in this were works by Tim Brown and by Roger L. Martin. See P. G. Rowe, *Design Thinking* (Cambridge, MA: MIT Press, 1987); T. Brown, "Design Thinking," *Harvard Business Review* 86, no. 6 (2008): 84–92; T. Brown, *Change by Design: How Design Thinking Transforms Organizations and Inspires Innovation* (New York: HarperCollins, 2009); and R. L. Martin, *The Design of Business: Why Design Thinking Is the Next Competitive Advantage* (Boston, MA: Harvard Business Press, 2009).
2. T. Kelley and D. Kelley, *Creative Confidence: Unleashing the Creative Potential within Us All* (New York: Crown Business, 2013).

8

Developing New Products in Emerging Markets

Srivardhini K. Jha, Ishwardutt Parulkar,
Rishikesha T. Krishnan, and Charles Dhanaraj

For more than a decade, multinational enterprises from developed countries have been moving a substantial part of their research and development (R&D) activity to emerging markets such as India and China. While the location of R&D centers in other *developed countries* has been driven by lucrative markets or specific expertise available in the local ecosystems of those countries, the location of R&D in *developing countries* has been driven largely by the availability of skilled manpower at low cost. At first, these R&D centers in emerging markets operated largely as extended arms of R&D in the home country, executing well-defined projects under close supervision from headquarters.

However, the dynamics of multinationals' R&D are rapidly changing. Emerging markets are new growth drivers of the global economy, and their unique bundle of opportunities and challenges can be a wellspring of innovation for a multinational company.[1] Simultaneously, many R&D centers in emerging markets have evolved to accumulate advanced technical capabilities, leading their employees to clamor for higher-value-added work and to seek responsibility for a complete product or technology. This clamor gets louder when the R&D subsidiary is located in a country with a large local market, such as India or China.

Given these trends, R&D subsidiaries in emerging markets are uniquely positioned to play an important role in multinational companies' innovation strategies. However, this thinking is often at odds with the dominant innovation mindset, structures, and processes within multinational companies based in developed countries. Also, the fact that the product leadership capabilities of R&D centers in emerging markets are often not well established within the multinational enterprise creates a higher hurdle. Against this backdrop, we explore several questions: When is the subsidiary ready to take on such responsibilities? What kinds of products or technology should the subsidiary work on? How should this be developed? While many companies have struggled with these issues, a successful innovation from Cisco Systems Inc.'s R&D unit in India—a family of mobile backhaul routers, named ASR 901 aggregation services routers—offers insights into these questions.[2]

About the Research

The research method employed for this study was a combination of quasi-participatory action research and the case study method. One of the authors, Ishwardutt Parulkar, was a core member of the ASR 901 project, intimately involved in every aspect of the project from conceptualization to commercialization. This author is also trained in the research tradition. Through the duration of the project, he took detailed notes about the project's challenges, dilemmas, and key decisions. At the end of the project, he authored a white paper to capture the important takeaways from the project.

We complemented this rich firsthand knowledge with an in-depth case study of the project. For the case study, we gathered data from multiple sources—key respondent interviews, company documents, and secondary data from external sources—in order to understand the evolution of Cisco India R&D from the time of its establishment to the initiation of the ASR 901 project, as well as the activities during the project itself.

We conducted 10 semistructured interviews encompassing all the key members of the ASR 901 team, the executives at the India R&D center, and the product champions at Cisco headquarters. This helped us gain multiple perspectives on the development of the product.

We wrote a detailed case study based on the information gathered from multiple sources of data. We had several extensive discussions with our practitioner author to ensure that the emerging framework accurately captured the innovation process, and we refined it as appropriate. We then distilled the important takeaways for managers.

The ASR 901 family of routers acts as the entry point for consumer voice and data into the mobile telecommunication network and sits in what is referred to as the "last mile" of the network.

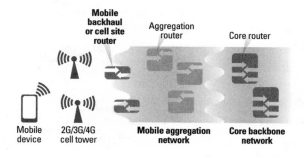

How a Telecom Network Is Structured

In a modern telecom network, the core backbone network consists of large routers connecting cities over very high-speed links; that core network is fed by aggregation networks that aggregate network traffic from cell towers in a geographical area. Cisco India saw an opportunity to develop a mobile backhaul router (also known as a cell site router) to link cell towers to the core telecom network.

ASR 901 was conceptualized and developed by Cisco's R&D center in India to serve the unique needs of emerging-market customers. However, the product also found traction in developed markets, making it a global product. The decisions taken with respect to the choice of ASR 901 as the product to be developed in India, its technological features, and its resourcing strategy provide valuable lessons for multinational managers both at headquarters and at subsidiaries on how to turn the company's emerging market presence into a source of innovation.

Decision #1: Key Enablers of Emerging-Market Innovation

Managers in emerging-country R&D outfits need to consider three key factors before they embark on innovation for local and similar markets. These enablers are the R&D capability of the unit, the size and uniqueness of the market opportunity, and the presence of executive champions, both at headquarters and at the subsidiary.

R&D Capability

First and foremost, the R&D unit needs to have well-developed R&D capabilities. This means the unit should have the breadth and depth of technical knowledge required to undertake complete product development. Without this capability, the unit will remain reliant on headquarters and other units within the company, which might unnecessarily prolong the process or end the project prematurely.

Leading up to ASR 901, Cisco India had built these capabilities to a large extent. In 1996, Cisco set up an R&D center in Bangalore, India. The center started with a handful of engineers working as an offshore, extended team of Cisco headquarters, executing specific tasks for one or two business units. The primary driver for setting up the center was the availability of a large pool of English-speaking engineering talent and low operating costs.

In the years following its establishment, the India center consistently met delivery and quality targets, attracting more investment from headquarters and increasing the scale of its R&D. At the same time, the center enhanced the depth and breadth of its technical capability, and by 2009, the center had filed more than 170 patents. The India center was given development ownership for certain product components, although product innovation continued to be driven by headquarters and oriented to the needs of the developed markets.

As the India R&D center matured, the R&D managers and staff aspired to innovate rather than simply execute; a culture of innovation and entrepreneurship emerged. More importantly, the center had accumulated most of the capabilities required to deliver on that aspiration.

Market Opportunity

As Cisco India's R&D matured, the Indian economy saw a major transformation in the telecom sector. As a result of deregulation in the 1990s, a number of telecom service providers (both domestic and foreign) entered the Indian market. The free-market forces triggered above-average growth, and the telecom subscriber base grew more than 20-fold in a decade, from under 28.5 million subscribers in 2000 to over 621 million in 2010.[3] To keep pace with this growth, telecom service provider investments in network infrastructure also grew sharply in India, going from $60.8 billion in 2007 to $89.6 billion in 2010, at a time when capital investments stayed fairly flat in developed markets.[4]

The market opportunity in India and other emerging markets was clearly big, and it was reflected in Cisco's strategy. In 2006, Cisco's then-CEO, John Chambers, announced that Bangalore would be developed as Cisco's Globalization Center East. The goal was to grow the Bangalore site to reach an equal technical footing with the company's headquarters in San Jose, California, to support Cisco's globalization strategy. To execute this ambitious goal, Cisco senior vice president of customer advocacy Wim Elfrink was appointed the company's chief globalization officer and relocated to Bangalore in 2007. As a result, the footprint of the India center, which had been predominantly an R&D organization, expanded. Cisco services—both technical and advanced—gained a strong presence in India. Sales, marketing, and supply chain management also grew.

Growth on multiple functional dimensions created a better dialogue between R&D in India and customer-facing teams. The R&D center started receiving feedback on the lack of appropriate products for the local market. It became increasingly evident that Indian and other emerging-market customers had unique requirements with respect to price, network scalability, subscriber monetization, and simultaneous support for legacy (2G) and 3G/4G network deployments. This created an impetus to innovate.

In sum, a large market opportunity combined with unique customer requirements is a key enabler of innovation for emerging markets. While most emerging markets do present a sizable market opportunity, it is the uniqueness of customer requirements that creates a compelling need to innovate.

Executive Champions

The third key prerequisite for innovation by subsidiaries in emerging markets is the support of executive champions, both at the subsidiary and at corporate headquarters. Leading an innovation effort from an emerging-country R&D center, especially one without an established track record, goes against the dominant mindset of many multinationals and presents many challenges. An executive champion who believes in the center's ability can mitigate these challenges.

Cisco India R&D had built credibility with key executives at the company's headquarters through its consistent performance over the years. Pankaj Patel, a senior vice president in Cisco R&D at the time, was a strong believer in the emerging-market opportunity and the capabilities of the India center. Wim Elfrink, Cisco's chief globalization officer, who was located in India at that time, was also a strong champion.

With support from these executive champions, Cisco India's R&D leadership in 2009 put up seed funding to explore opportunities in emerging markets. The funds supported two key staff positions—a chief technical architect and a product manager—bridging the skill gaps at the India R&D center and creating the core team for new initiatives.

In sum, Cisco India's R&D had all three enablers of innovation in place: a critical mass of end-to-end product development capability, a growing market with unique needs, and executive champions. It is easy to see how an innovation initiative would falter without any one of these three factors. Without advanced technical capabilities, it would be impossible to architect and lead product development. Without a unique market opportunity, there is no business case. Without executive champions, it would be difficult to mobilize resources and find traction within the company. Therefore, R&D managers need to evaluate where they stand vis-à-vis these factors before embarking on innovation in and for emerging markets.

Decision #2: What Product to Develop?

Once the key enabling factors are in place, the next step is to identify a suitable product to develop. This demands careful consideration of market needs and an assessment of both internal capabilities and the overall fit of the chosen product and its category with the company's product portfolio. While the actual product will vary depending on the industry, attention to these three factors increases the chance of success.

Market Need

The product has to address an important need that customers in emerging markets have. The core team at Cisco met with customers in emerging markets to understand their needs and pain points. Cisco found that the mobile subscriber explosion in emerging markets was fueling rapid capacity expansion by service providers. At one point in 2009, India was adding about 15 million new mobile subscribers a month. The number of cell sites was expected to grow rapidly in such markets: The technology market intelligence company ABI Research predicted that by 2014, 39% of all cell towers would be located in the Asia-Pacific region. These trends indicated that there was an opportunity to develop a mobile backhaul router (also known as a cell site router) that links cell towers to the core telecom network.[5]

Portfolio Fit

The product should also fill a gap in the company's product portfolio. This will generate new revenue streams and increase the chance of internal support for the product. A modern telecom network is hierarchical, with the core backbone network of large routers connecting cities over very high-speed links; the core network is fed by networks that aggregate traffic from cell towers in a geographical area such as a metropolitan zone. In 2009, Cisco was a strong player in the "core" and "aggregation" layers of the service provider network, but it was less dominant in the mobile backhaul router segment, which had a few strong competitors. Therefore, a product for this segment seemed to be complementary to the company's existing portfolio.

Further, the pattern of network evolution in India and other emerging markets imposed some unique requirements on the product. Mobile backhaul was moving from the prevalent 2G technology for voice to 3G/4G technologies for data and broadband. However, even with the deployment of 3G/4G, legacy (2G) systems persisted, as voice was still a large source of revenue for telecoms in India. Therefore, the proposed router had to be versatile enough to support existing 2G services as well as to handle rapid scalability to the next-generation 3G/4G mobile backhaul technology.

Product Capability Fit

The product should ideally be one that is reasonably complex, but also one that builds on the capabilities of the subsidiary and that can be developed within a relatively short period. A product of low complexity would not work as a compelling proof point to demonstrate the subsidiary's product development capability. At the same time, a very complex product would take too long, which would test the patience of headquarters. The project might even run out of steam before the R&D center could develop a working prototype and validate demand.

The aforementioned attributes helped the core team arrive at a product that could be developed from the India R&D center. Cisco India decided to develop a family of routers, the ASR 901, for last-mile access in mobile backhaul of telecom networks. Essentially, these routers would be the entry point for consumer mobile voice and data from the cell towers into the telecom network. For Cisco India, a product for last-mile access in mobile backhaul was something that could be developed in 12–18 months and also filled a critical product portfolio need.

Decision #3: How to Develop the Product?

Once a suitable product has been identified, the next step is to develop a working prototype, followed by the end product, which is fully functional, is extensively tested and qualified, and can be manufactured in volume. Product development is a resource-intensive activity, requiring head count, equipment, and other infrastructure. At this stage, there are generally two options that subsidiary managers can pursue.

The first option is to present the business case for the identified product to headquarters and secure necessary resources to undertake prototype and product development. In this approach, the development of the product will have the full support of the organization. However, with multiple proposals for products in different market segments competing for resources, there is a chance that the proposal may not be supported. This is especially true in the case of unproven product development capability and an untested emerging market. The second approach is to develop the prototype with locally available resources and demonstrate product development capability and commercial viability. In this approach, garnering the necessary level of resources may be a challenge. Furthermore, any unforeseen challenges and delays may compromise the viability of the project due to its limited resources and acceptance within the company.

The Decision Matrix

We have developed a decision matrix to provide a general framework for choosing one approach over the other.

The horizontal axis captures the relative strategic importance of a given geographic market to the company vis-à-vis other markets, which could be high or low. The vertical axis is project specific and captures the nature of the business case for the proposed product.

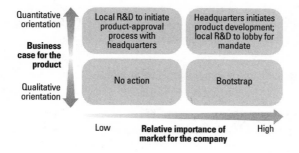

A Decision Matrix for Product Development by a Subsidiary

When deciding how to best proceed with an idea for a new product, managers at subsidiaries of multinational companies should consider two important factors: (1) whether the business case for the new product is primarily quantitative or qualitative; and (2) the relative importance of the geographic market to the parent company.

The business case may have a strong quantitative orientation, which means it would include hard metrics such as investment dollars, total addressable market, estimated market share, estimated revenue for one to three years, and return on investment. A qualitative business case, on the other hand, would stress factors such as mind share in a new market, gaining early-entrant status, countering growing competitor dominance in an emerging market, and the total addressable market over a longer period. Of course, every business case will have both quantitative and qualitative elements, but this dimension identifies which one predominates. When the business case is quantitatively oriented, it is easier to communicate and garner support than when it is qualitatively oriented.

When the relative importance of the geographic market for a company is high, it can be assumed that the company is well attuned to the market's trends and requirements. Therefore, any such product with a quantitatively strong business case (top-right quadrant) is likely to be on headquarters' radar and to get into the development pipeline.[6] In this case, the local R&D center has to compete with other R&D centers in the company to take ownership for developing the product. If there is a quantitatively strong business case for a product, the local R&D unit has a good chance of convincing headquarters to invest. Therefore, initiating the standard product approval process with headquarters would be the preferred option (top-left quadrant). However, it is possible that the business case has a qualitative orientation because the opportunity is still nascent. In this case, even if the market is important for the company, the opportunity may not be immediately apparent. The local R&D unit, by virtue of its proximity to the market, is more likely to be in tune with such emergent requirements. But the qualitative orientation of the business case makes it difficult to quantify the return on investment and get product development approved by headquarters. In such cases (bottom-right), the R&D center needs to creatively mobilize resources to develop a working prototype. We refer to this as "bootstrapping." Finally, if the relative importance of the geographic market is low and the business case is qualitative (bottom-left), it is better to wait until there is a more quantitative business case or there is a strategic shift toward the market within the company.

Cisco India's mobile backhaul router for last-mile access mapped onto the bottom-right quadrant of the decision matrix. Even though India was an important market for Cisco, as evidenced by the establishment of the globalization center in India, the business case for the proposed router would not have met some of the quantitative thresholds typically needed to successfully get through Cisco's companywide R&D project-commit process. However, the router project presented a qualitatively strong business case: The product addressed a pressing customer need, filled a critical gap in the company's portfolio, and aspired to open up a segment where competitors were rapidly gaining a foothold in an important market. Therefore, the core team in India decided to take a bootstrapping approach (bottom-right in the matrix) to develop the prototype. This novel approach to product development provides an alternative to the more common structured product development process within companies.

Bootstrapping

The core team, comprising the chief technical architect and the product manager, realized that it would be difficult to start the development of ASR 901 through Cisco's structured R&D project-commit process. They needed to bootstrap by cobbling together the limited resources at their disposal to build a prototype and successively work their way toward broader acceptance within the company. This strategy had to be executed on multiple fronts to mobilize the key resources required for development.

In addition to the chief technical architect, the team needed a few senior technologists with expertise in specific domains to design state-of-the-art, complex features and provide general technical direction to the rest of the engineering team. However, there was a shortage of domain experts, especially in some of the advanced networking protocols, and hiring from outside was difficult and expensive. The team instead bridged the domain expertise gap by borrowing a handful of senior engineers handpicked from other business units in India. This was possible because several groups had developed advanced technical capabilities in specific technology areas over the years. Further, since the success of the project was important for establishing the product development capabilities of the India R&D center, other engineering organizations within the company's operations in India were forthcoming in offering resources to help the project get off the ground. This arrangement also kept the costs down and stretched the modest seed funding the team was given. However, the technology implemented was cutting edge and adhered to global standards.

To build a prototype, the engineering team had to be staffed up considerably. With minimal seed funding at its disposal, the team decided to engage with an engineering services partner. The service partner would execute part of the development effort through a new revenue-sharing model. Instead of the traditional time and materials model, where payment is made at the time the services are provided, the new model involved payment as a percentage of revenue as the product started selling.

This new revenue-sharing model had several advantages. First, it deferred the nonrecurring engineering cost to a future date when the product had wider acceptance within the company, thereby stretching the minimal seed funds available. Second, it helped develop deeper partnerships with local companies and strengthen the local ecosystem through technology transfer. Third, it was a much faster way of staffing the team than hiring from the market. Fourth, the services partner had "more skin in the game" and worked as an integral part of the team, which was essential for a new product development effort.

ASR 901 product development involved working across the entire stack of technologies—silicon chips, platform hardware, platform software, network operating system, and network management—and having them closely interface with each other. Many of these technologies were developed within Cisco, some came from suppliers as off-the-shelf components, and other portions were codeveloped with partners.

For codevelopment, physical proximity and constant engagement with the partners was extremely important. However, most of the partners did not have a significant presence in India, and the handful of people who were locally available did not have the in-depth technical expertise to work with Cisco on a complex, next-generation product like ASR 901.

There were two particular touch points when close interaction was critical. First was at the time of architecting the product, when it was important to understand the chip's capabilities and all its nuances, to be able to clearly define the hardware/software interfaces. Second was the "bring-up" phase, when the functionality of the prototype was tested for the first time, and intimate understanding of the silicon component and the hardware/software interface was critical. Working with partners halfway around the world was not viable.

To overcome this hurdle, the team leveraged Cisco's long-standing relationship with its suppliers. The team, through its champions at headquarters, was able to convince the key suppliers to staff up in India in order to support the development of ASR 901. The suppliers moved some key personnel to India, and this essentially plugged the gap in the hardware ecosystem for the development of ASR 901.

In sum, the team creatively mobilized all types of resources necessary for prototype development. It worked like a startup within a large company. The hierarchy was kept to a minimum, and all the engineers—Cisco employees as well as engineers from the partner organization—worked in a common workspace. This facilitated impromptu whiteboard discussions and quick resolution of questions and issues. The junior engineers were guided by the senior engineers and received immediate feedback on pieces of code and design. This setup facilitated rapid learning and quick resolution of issues through joint problem solving. Further, close interactions with the partner organization gave the team ample exposure to technical constraints and trade-offs. As the team members designed and developed the product prototype, they constantly challenged entrenched design norms to meet the stringent product requirements of emerging-market customers with respect to cost, power, and form factor, while simultaneously advancing the state of the art in mobile backhaul technology. With this setup, the team was able to build a working prototype within six months.

The effort shows that bootstrapping can be a viable alternative to the standard corporate prototype development process that involves getting upfront commitment to a concept. The specific activities involved in bootstrapping will depend on the industry in which the company operates and the nature of the product

Bootstrapping can be a viable alternative to the standard corporate prototype development process that involves getting upfront commitment to a concept.

being developed. However, the Cisco experience provides some general guidelines to managers on the types of organizational arrangements that can be structured to build a prototype on a shoestring budget.

Integration into Mainstream Development

Once a working prototype is in place, managers can demonstrate the technical and commercial viability of the product to all stakeholders within the company. They can also showcase the prototype to select customers for early feedback and assess the level of interest in the product. If the prototype is well received by internal and external stakeholders, the business case is made, which paves the way for full-scale development.

The ASR 901 prototype started getting attention from customer-facing organizations in the company. The active engagement of the core team with customer-facing groups resulted in a slow but sure realization that the product filled a gap in the company's portfolio. This provided market validation for ASR 901. Importantly, the product gained excellent traction with some key customers in the developed markets because it offered leading technology features at attractive cost, power, and form-factor-design points. For example, low power consumption, which was critical to containing operating expenses in emerging markets, found an additional application in the developed markets, where corporations have a social responsibility mandate to be "green" in addition to delivering economic benefits.

The team now had a working prototype along with a demonstrated business case, thanks to customer interest in emerging and developed markets. The validation of the concept cleared the way for "execution commit" from the company. Headquarters sanctioned the next round of funding, which went toward staffing up the engineering teams and building the large number of prototypes required for full-fledged testing and qualification.

As a result of these developments, the product became part of the mainstream engineering organization. With formal recognition and funding, the team aligned itself with Cisco's standard product development process and was able to leverage domain expertise from other teams to complete the development and qualification and enter trials with early customers.

The Transformation of Cisco India

ASR 901 was launched in October 2011. Over the next year, several variants of ASR 901 were developed and sold to more than 100 customers in 46 countries. The product improved on the state of the art in some of the key emerging mobile backhaul technology areas. It achieved this with significant improvements in cost, power, and footprint efficiencies, which met the stringent requirements of emerging markets while greatly appealing to developed markets. The success of the project was one of the factors that contributed to the formation of a new Cisco business unit, Provider Access Business Unit (PABU), centered in India.

The market success, strengthening of product development capability, and organizational evolution led to a string of new products from Cisco India over the next few years. In December 2014, Cisco showcased three new communications products conceptualized, architected, and designed in India.

In 2015, Pankaj Patel, then executive vice president and chief development officer at Cisco, summarized the transformation of Cisco India: "We came to India for the costs, we stayed for the quality, we invested for innovation, and now we are creating a new industry."[7]

Notes

1. "The World Turned Upside Down," *The Economist*, April 15, 2010.

2. See http://www.cisco.com.

3. Telecom Regulatory Authority of India, "TRAI Annual Report 2009–2010," November 9, 2010, http://www.trai.gov.in/about-us/annual-reports.

4. KPMG and Federation of Indian Chambers of Commerce and Industry, "m-Powering India," December 7–9, 2011, https://www.kpmg.de/docs/mPowering_India_2011.pdf.

5. Backhaul of a telecommunications network comprises the intermediate links between the core network and the small subnetworks at the edge of the entire hierarchical network. Definition from J. Salmelin and E. Metsälä, "Mobile Backhaul" (Chichester, UK: John Wiley & Sons, 2012).

6. V. Govindarajan and C. Trimble, *Reverse Innovation: Create Far from Home, Win Everywhere* (Boston, MA: Harvard Business Press, 2012).

7. "Bangalore R&D Unit Key to Us; Has Filed 800-Plus Patents: Cisco," *Economic Times*, February 8, 2015, https://economictimes.indiatimes.com/tech/ites/bangalore-rd-unit-key-to-us-has-filed-800-plus-patents-cisco/articleshow/46162939.cms.

Managing the Challenges

9

The Hard Truth about Business Model Innovation

Clayton M. Christensen, Thomas Bartman,
and Derek van Bever

Surveying the landscape of recent attempts at business model innovation, one could be forgiven for believing that success is essentially random. For example, conventional wisdom would suggest that Google Inc., with its Midas touch for innovation, might be more likely to succeed in its business model innovation efforts than a traditional, mature, industrial company like the automaker Daimler AG. But that's not always the case. Google+, which Google launched in 2011, has failed to gain traction as a social network, while at this writing Daimler is building a promising new venture, car2go, which has become one of the world's leading car-sharing businesses. Are those surprising outcomes simply anomalies, or could they have been predicted?

To our eyes, the landscape of failed attempts at business model innovation is crowded—and becoming more so—as management teams at established companies mount both offensive and defensive initiatives involving new business models. A venture capitalist who advises large financial services companies on strategy shared his observation about the anxiety his investors feel about the changes underway in their industry: "They look at the fintech [financial technology] startups and see their business models being unbundled and attacked at every point in the value chain." And financial services companies are not alone. A PwC survey published in 2015 revealed that 54% of CEOs worldwide were concerned about new competitors entering their market, and an equal percentage said they had either begun to compete in nontraditional markets themselves or considered doing so.[1] For its part, the Boston Consulting Group reports that in a 2014 survey of 1,500 senior executives, 94% stated that their companies had attempted some degree of business model innovation.[2]

We've decided to wade in at this juncture because business model innovation is too important to be left to random chance and guesswork. Executed correctly, it has the ability to make companies resilient in the face of change and to create growth unbounded by the limits of existing businesses. Further, we have seen businesses overcome other management problems that resulted in high failure rates. For example, if you bought a car in the United States in the 1970s, there was a very real possibility that you would get a "lemon." Some cars were inexplicably afflicted by problem after problem, to the point that it was accepted that such lemons were a natural consequence of inherent randomness in manufacturing. But management expert W. Edwards Deming demonstrated that manufacturing doesn't have to be random, and, having incorporated his insights in the 1980s, the major automotive companies have made lemons a memory of a bygone era. To our eyes, there are currently a lot of lemons being produced by the business model innovation process—but it doesn't have to be that way.

In our experience, when the business world encounters an intractable management problem, it's a sign that business executives and scholars are getting something wrong—that there isn't yet a satisfactory theory for what's causing the problem, and under what circumstances it can be overcome. This is what has resulted in so much wasted time and effort in attempts at corporate renewal. And this confusion has spawned a welter of well-meaning but ultimately misguided advice, ranging from prescriptions to innovate only close to the core business to assertions about the type of leader who is able to pull off business model transformations, or the capabilities a business requires to achieve successful business model innovation.

The hard truth about business model innovation is that it is not the attributes of the innovator that principally drive success or failure, but rather the nature of the innovation being attempted. Business models develop through predictable stages over time—and executives need to understand the priorities associated with each business model stage. Business leaders then need to evaluate whether or not a business model innovation they are considering is consistent with the current priorities of their existing business model. This analysis matters greatly, as it drives a whole host of decisions about where the new initiative should be housed, how its performance should be measured, and how the resources and processes at work in the company will either support it or extinguish it.

This truth has revealed itself to us gradually over time, but our thinking has crystallized over the past two years in an intensive study effort we have led at the Harvard Business School. As part of that research effort, we have analyzed 26 cases of both successful and failed business model innovation; in addition, we have selected a set of nine industry-leading companies whose senior leaders are currently struggling with the issue of conceiving and sustaining success in business model innovation.

About the Research

This article assembles knowledge that the primary author has developed over the course of two decades studying what causes good businesses to fail, complemented by a two-year intensive research project to uncover where current managers and leadership teams stumble in executing business model innovation. Over the course of the past two years of in-depth study, we evaluated 26 business model innovations in the historical record that had run a course from idea to development to success, or failure. The study identified 10 failures and 16 successes and coded each across 20 dimensions to identify patterns associated with success and failure.

To further develop our understanding of the causality behind the relationships we observed, we also assembled a cohort of nine market-leading companies from industries as diverse as information technology, consumer products, travel and leisure, fashion, publishing, and financial services. Each of these companies is attempting to execute some degree of business model innovation. We observed these companies as they undertook their business model innovation efforts and conducted interviews with more than 60 C-level executives across the nine companies. In addition to our interviews, we convened two working sessions at Harvard Business School that brought executives from each company together to discuss the challenges, opportunities, and realities of business model innovation from the perspective of the manager.

We have profiled these nine companies' efforts extensively, documented their successes and failures, and convened their executives on campus periodically to enable them to share insights and frustrations with each other. Stepping back, we've made a number of observations that we hope will prove generally helpful, and we also have a sense of the work that remains to be done.

There are a number of lessons that managers can learn from past successes and failures, but all depend on understanding the rules that govern business model formation and development—how new models are created and how they evolve across time, the kinds of changes that are possible to those models at various stages of development, and what that means for organizational renewal and growth.

The Business Model's Journey

The confusion surrounding business model innovation begins, appropriately enough, with confusion about the term "business model." In our course at the Harvard Business School, we teach students to use a four-box business model framework that we developed with colleagues from the consulting firm Innosight LLC. This framework consists of the *value proposition* for customers (which we will refer to as the "job to be done"); the organization's *resources*, such as people, cash, and technology; the *processes* that it uses to convert inputs to finished products or services; and the profit formula that dictates the margins, asset velocity, and scale required to achieve an attractive return.[3,4] Collectively, the organization's resources and processes define its capabilities—how it does things—while its customer value proposition and *profit formula* characterize its priorities—what it does, and why.[5]

This way of viewing business models is useful for two reasons. First, it supplies a common language and framework to understand the capabilities of a business. Second, it highlights the interdependencies among elements and illuminates what a business is *in*capable of doing. Interdependencies describe the integration required between individual elements of the business model—each component of the model must be congruent with the others. They explain why, for example, Rolls-Royce Motor

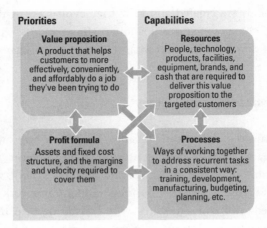

The Elements of a Business Model

A business model is made up of four elements: (1) a value proposition for customers; (2) resources, such as people, money, and technology; (3) the processes that the organization uses to convert inputs to finished products or services; and (4) the profit formula that dictates the margins, asset velocity, and scale required to achieve an attractive return. Inter-dependencies, represented here by bidirectional arrows, describe the integration required between individual elements of the business model. They require that every component of the model be congruent with every other component.

Cars Ltd. is unable to sell cheap bespoke cars and why Wal-Mart Stores Inc. is unable to combine low prices with fancy stores.

Understanding the interdependencies in a business model is important because those interdependencies grow and harden across time, creating another fundamental truth that is critical for leaders to understand: *Business models by their very nature are designed not to change, and they become less flexible and more resistant to change as they develop over time.* Leaders of the world's best businesses should take special note, because the better your business model performs at its assigned task, the more interdependent and less capable of change it likely is. The strengthening of these interdependencies is not an intentional act by managers; rather, it comes from the emergence of processes that arise as the natural, collective response to recurrent activities. The longer a business unit exists, the more often it will confront similar problems and the more ingrained its approaches to solving those problems will become. We often refer to these ingrained approaches as a business's "culture."[6]

In fact, this pattern is so consistent and important that we've begun to think of the development of a business model across time as resembling a journey whose progress and route are predictable—although the time that it takes a business model to follow this journey will differ by industry and circumstance.

As the diagram depicts, a business model, which in an established company is typically embodied in a business unit, travels a one-way journey, beginning with the creation of the new business unit and its business model, then shifting to sustaining and growing the business unit, and ultimately moving to wringing efficiency from it.[7] Each stage of the journey supports a specific type of innovation, builds a particular set of interdependencies into the model, and is responsive to a particular set

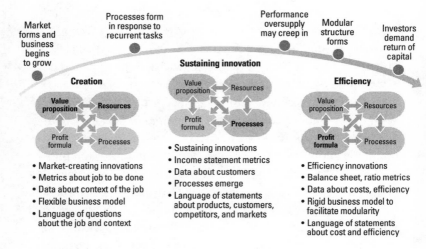

The Three Stages of a Business Model's Journey

A business model, which in an established company is typically embodied in a business unit, travels a journey that begins with the creation of the new business unit and its business model, and then shifts to sustaining and growing the business unit—and still later to wringing efficiency from it. Each stage of the journey is conducive to a specific type of innovation, builds a particular set of interdependencies into the model, and is responsive to a particular set of performance metrics. Green bidirectional arrows represent interdependencies between aspects of the business model that are well established at that stage; business model elements in bold represent areas of focus during that stage of business model evolution. Business model elements and interdependencies shown in beige are still somewhat flexible at that point in the journey.

of performance metrics. This is the arc of the journey of virtually every business model—if it is lucky and successful enough to travel the entire length of the route. Unsuccessful business units will falter before concluding the journey and be absorbed or shuttered. Now, let's explore each of the three stages and how the business model evolves through them.

Stage 1: Creation

Peter Drucker once said that the purpose of a business is to create a customer.[8] That goal characterizes the first stage of the journey, when the business searches for a meaningful value proposition, which it can design initial product and service offerings to fulfill. This is the stage at which a relatively small band of resources (a founding team armed with an idea, some funding and ambition, and sometimes a technology) is entirely focused on developing a compelling value proposition—fulfilling a significant unmet need, or "job."[9] It's useful to think of the members of the founding team as completely immersed in this search. The information swirling around them at this point in the journey—the information they pay the most attention to—consists of insights they are able to glean into the unfulfilled jobs of prospective customers.

We emphasize the primacy of the job at this point of the journey because it is very difficult for a business to remain focused on a customer's job as the operation scales. Understanding the progress a customer is trying to make—and providing the experiences in purchase and use that will fulfill that job perfectly—requires patient, bottom-up inquiry. The language that is characteristic of this stage is the language of questions, not of answers. The link between value proposition and resources is already forming, but the rest of the model is still unformed: The new organization has yet to face the types of recurrent tasks that create processes, and its profit formula is nascent and exploratory. This gives the business an incredible flexibility that will disappear as it evolves along the journey and its language shifts from questions to answers.

Stage 2: Sustaining Innovation

Business units lucky and skilled enough to discover an unfulfilled job and develop a product or service that addresses it enter the sustaining innovation phase of the business model journey. At this stage, customer demand reaches the point where the greatest challenge the business faces is no longer determining whether the product fulfills a job, but rather scaling operations to meet growing demand. Whereas in the creation phase the business unit created customers, in the sustaining innovation phase it is building these customers into a reliable, loyal base and building the organization into a well-oiled machine that delivers the product or service flawlessly and repeatedly. The innovations characteristic of this phase of the business model journey are what we call sustaining innovations—in other words, better products that can be sold for higher prices to the current target market.

A curious change sets in at this stage of the journey, however: As the business unit racks up sales, the voice of the customer gets louder, drowning out to some extent the voice of the job. Why does this happen? It's not that managers intend to lose touch with the job, but while the voice of the job is faint and requires interrogation to hear, the voice of the customer is transmitted into the business with each sale and gets louder with every additional transaction. The voice of the job emerges only in one-to-one, in-depth conversations that reveal the job's context in a customer's life, but listening to the voice of the customer allows the business to scale its understanding. Customers can be surveyed and polled to learn their preferences, and those preferences are then channeled into efforts to improve existing products.

The business unit is now no longer in the business of identifying new unmet needs but rather in the business of building processes—locking down the current model. The data that surrounds managers is now about revenues, products, customers, and competition. While in the creation phase, the founding team had to dig to discover data, data now floods the business's offices, with more arriving with each new transaction. Data begs to be analyzed—it is the way the game is scored—so the influx of data precipitates the adoption of metrics to evaluate the business's performance and direct future activity to improving the metrics. The performance metrics in this phase focus on the income statement, leading managers to direct investments toward growing the top line and maximizing the bottom line.

Stage 3: Efficiency

At some point, however, these investments in product performance no longer generate adequate additional profitability. At this point, the business unit begins to prioritize the activities of efficiency innovation, which reduce cost by eliminating labor or by redesigning products to eliminate components or replace them with cheaper alternatives. (There is, however, always some amount of both types of innovation—sustaining and efficiency—occurring at any point of a business's evolution.) Broadly, the activities of efficiency innovation include outsourcing, adding financial leverage, optimizing processes, and consolidating industries to gain economies of scale. While many factors can cause businesses to transition into the efficiency innovation phase of their evolution, one we have often observed is the result of performance "overshoot," in which the business delivers more performance than the market can utilize and consumers become unwilling to pay for additional performance improvement or to upgrade to improved versions. Managers should not bemoan the shift to efficiency innovation. It needs to happen; over time, business units must become more efficient to remain competitive, and the shift to efficiency innovations as the predominant form of innovation activity is a natural outcome of that process.

To managers, the efficiency innovation phase marks the point where the voice of the shareholders drowns out the voice of the customer. Gleaning new understanding of that initial job to be done is now the long-lost ambition of a bygone era, and managers become inundated with data about costs and efficiency. The business unit frequently achieves efficiency by shifting to a modular structure, standardizing the interdependencies between each of the components of its business model so that they may be outsourced to third parties. In hardening these interdependencies, the business unit reaps the efficiency rewards of modularization but leaves flexibility behind, firmly cementing the structure of its business model in place. Deviations from the existing structure undermine the modularity of the components and reduce efficiency, so when evaluating such changes, the business will often choose to forsake them in pursuit of greater efficiency.

Now, when the business unit generates increasing amounts of free cash flow from its efficiency innovations, it is likely to sideline the capital, to diversify the company, or to invest it in industry consolidation. This is one of the major drivers of mergers and acquisitions (M&A) activity. Whereas the sustaining innovation phase was exciting to managers, customers, and shareholders, the efficiency innovation phase reduces degrees of managerial freedom. Efficiency innovations lure managers with their promises of low risk, high returns, and quick paybacks from cost reduction, but the end result is often a race to the bottom that sees the business's ability to serve the job and customers atrophy as it improves its service to shareholders.

The natural evolution of business units occurs all around us. Consider the case of The Boeing Co. and its wildly successful 737 business unit. The 737 business was announced in 1965 and launched its first version, the 737-100, in 1967, with Lufthansa as its first customer. With orders from several additional major airlines, the new business unit demonstrated that its medium-haul plane fulfilled an important job to be done. Before even delivering the first -100, Boeing began improving the 737 and launched a stretched version, the -200, with a longer fuselage to meet demands from airlines requiring greater seating capacity. Boeing entered the sustaining innovation phase and continued to improve its product by developing several generations of new 737s, stretching the fuselage like an accordion while nearly doubling the plane's range and more than doubling its revenue per available seat mile. The business continued to improve how it served customers with the Next Generation series in the 1990s, which offered even bigger aircraft and better avionics systems.

Facing increased competition and demands for improved financial performance, the 737 business shifted its focus to efficiency innovation in the early 2000s. To free resources and liberate capital, Boeing began to outsource aspects of 737 production.

Most notably, Boeing sold a facility in Wichita, Kansas, that manufactured the main fuselage platform for the 737 to the Toronto-based investment company Onex Corp. in 2005. Outsourcing subsystem production allowed the business to improve its capital efficiency and deliver improved returns on capital.[10]

Given that road map, what is the hope for companies that seek to develop new business models or to create new businesses? Thus far in this chapter we've explored the journey that business units take over time. And while we're not sure that a business unit can break off from this race, we know that its parent companies can—by developing new businesses. Although the processes of an individual business unit's business model propel it along this journey, the opportunity exists to develop a process of business creation at the corporate level. But doing so successfully requires paying careful attention to the implications of the business model road map.

Implications for Business Model Innovation

It's worth internalizing the road map view of business model evolution because it helps explain why most attempts to alter the course of existing business units fail. Unaware of the interdependencies and rigidities that constrain business units to pursuing their existing journey, managers attempt to compel existing business units to pursue new priorities or attempt to create a new business inside an existing unit. Using the road map as a guiding principle allows leaders to correctly categorize the innovation opportunities that appear before them in terms of their fit with their existing business model's priorities. Several recommendations for managers emerge from this insight.

The only types of innovation you can perform naturally within an existing business model are those that build on and improve the existing model and accelerate its progress.

Determine how consistent the opportunity is with the priorities of the existing business model. The only types of innovation you can perform naturally within an existing business model are those that build on and improve the existing model and accelerate its progress along the journey—in other words, those innovations that are consistent with its current priorities—by sharpening its focus on fulfilling the existing job or improving its financial performance. Therefore, a crucial question for leaders to ask when evaluating an innovation opportunity is: To what degree does it align with the existing priorities of the business model?

Many failed business model innovations involve the pursuit of opportunities that appear to be consistent with a unit's current business model but that in fact are likely to be rejected by the existing business or its customers.

Evaluating the Fit between an Opportunity and an Existing Business

Determining whether an opportunity aligns to a business's existing priorities is not an exact science, but there are questions that managers should ask to gauge how closely an opportunity aligns to the existing priorities. The greater the degree of alignment, the better it is to pursue the opportunity through the existing business; conversely, the greater the difference, the more necessary it will be to pursue the opportunity through a separate, dedicated business unit that has the autonomy to develop a unique business model to fulfill those objectives.

In the Creation Stage

In this phase, the entirety of the business unit's focus should be dedicated to understanding the primary business, accomplished through discovery of the job to be done and "pivoting" of the business model to effectively fulfill the functional, emotional, and social attributes of that job or a superior unfulfilled job that is discovered.

In the Sustaining Innovation Stage

In this phase, managers should evaluate the fit between the opportunity and the existing business unit on the basis of the consistency with the existing unit's job to be done and the effect on its income statement. Questions managers should ask include the following:

Does the innovation opportunity...

- improve our ability to better serve the existing job to be done, in similar circumstances in customers' lives?
- grow our current addressable market or bring new customers into our market?
- improve our revenue growth, profitability, or margins?
- help us make more money in the way we are structured to make money?

In the Efficiency Stage

When the business unit is focused on efficiency, managers should evaluate the fit between innovation opportunities and the existing business by the impact on the balance sheet. Questions managers should ask include the following:

Does the innovation opportunity...

- enable us to serve our existing customers with lower costs?
- allow us to use our capital more efficiently?
- allow us to liberate capital currently invested in the value chain?
- enable us to modularize our offering to facilitate outsourcing and other partnerships for noncore elements of the model?

To determine how consistent an opportunity is with the priorities of the existing business model, leaders should ask: Is the new job to be done for the customer similar to the existing job? (The greater the similarity, the more appropriate it is for the existing business to pursue the opportunity.) How does pursuit of the opportunity affect the existing profit formula? Are the margins better, transaction sizes larger, and addressable markets bigger? If so, it is likely to fit well with the existing profit formula. If not, managers should proceed with caution in asking an existing business to take it on—and should instead consider creating a separate unit to pursue the new business model.

This distinction helps explain the performance of the two innovations with which we opened this chapter. Google saw Google+ as an extension of its search business and chose to integrate Google+ into its existing products and business. Google+ accounts were integrated into other Google products, and the business saw the incorporation of information from users' social networks as a way to generate improved, tailored search results. Viewed through the lens of Google's business model, a social network allowed the business to generate greater revenue and profitability by better targeting advertisements and delivering more advertisements through increased usage of its product platform. However, consumers apparently didn't see the value from combining search and social networking; to the consumer, the jobs are very different and arise in different circumstances in their lives. So, while Google maintains its exceptional search business, its social network failed to gain momentum.

Contrast Google's experience to that of Daimler, which recognized that car2go was a very different business and established it far afield from the home office and existing business. Daimler started car2go as an experiment tested by its employees working in Ulm, Germany. It housed the business in a corporate incubator that does not report to the existing consumer automotive businesses and designed it from the outset to fulfill Daimler's core job of providing mobility, but without the need to convince consumers to purchase vehicles. Recognizing that the priorities of a business that rents cars by the minute are very different from those involved in selling luxury vehicles, Daimler has kept car2go separate and allowed it to develop a unique business model capable of fulfilling its job profitably. However, car2go benefits from Daimler's ownership by using corporate resources where appropriate—for example, car2go rents vehicles only in the Daimler portfolio, principally the Smart Fortwo.

To achieve successful business model innovation, focus on creating new business models, rather than changing existing ones. As business model interdependencies arise, the ability to create new businesses within existing business units is lost. The resources and processes that work so perfectly in their original business model do so because they have been honed and optimized for delivering on the priorities of that model. The classic example of this was the movie rental company Blockbuster LLC, which attempted to develop a new DVD-by-mail business in response to the rise of Netflix Inc. by integrating that offering with its existing store network. This "bricks-and-clicks" combination made perfect sense to Blockbuster's managers, but what became obvious only in hindsight was that the two models would be at war with each other—the asset velocity required to maintain a profitable store network was incompatible with the DVD-by-mail offering. The paradox that managers must confront is that the specialized capabilities that are highly valuable to their current business model will tend to be unsuitable for, or even run counter to, the new business model.

Building a Business Creation Engine

For some time, we've argued that companies should build a business creation engine, capable of turning out a steady stream of innovative new business models, but to date no company we know of has built an enduring capability like that. We think that such an engine of sustained growth would quickly prove to be a company's most valuable asset, providing growth and creating new markets. But unleashing this growth potential requires very different behaviors than those required to successfully exploit existing markets.

The challenge, as the journey metaphor we've developed here should make clear, is that what is necessary is to turn an *event*—the act of creating a new business and a new business model—into a repeatable *process* at the corporate level. It must be a process because events are discrete activities with definitive start and end points, whereas processes are continuous and dynamic. Learnings from a previous event do not naturally or easily flow to subsequent events, causing the same mistakes to be repeated over and over. In contrast, processes by their nature can be learning opportunities that incorporate in future attempts what was discovered in previous iterations. Enacted as a process, the act of creation will improve over time and refine its ability to discover unfulfilled customer jobs and create new markets; the success rate will improve alongside the process, creating a virtuous cycle of growth.

While we have not discovered a perfect exemplar of this discipline, we have been tracking the efforts of some leading companies that are intent on building such a capability. While it is too early to hold any of them up as success stories, we can nonetheless discern five approaches that we believe have the potential to lead to success. Let's look at each of these approaches in turn.

Spot future growth gaps by understanding where each of your business units is on the journey. In our course at Harvard Business School, we teach students to use a tool called the *aggregate project plan* to allocate funding to different types of innovation.[11] Such a plan categorizes innovations by their distance from existing products and markets and specifies a desired allocation of funding to each bucket. We see application for this tool here as well.

The innovation team at Carolinas HealthCare System, a not-for-profit health care organization based in Charlotte, North Carolina, performed this type of analysis and identified a need to field additional innovation efforts that reflected the organization's belief that hospitals will be less central in the health care system of the future. Armed with this view, Carolinas HealthCare System has been able to plan innovation activity by type, ensuring that the organization invests appropriately across all three categories of the business model journey. As Dr. Jean Wright, chief innovation officer at Carolinas HealthCare System, said, "The strength of the journey framework is that it allowed us to see that our investments in business creation are very different from our investments in our existing businesses. More importantly, it has helped us see that both types are important."

Run with potential disruptors of your business. Another approach is to create incentives and channels for entrepreneurs to bring new and, in some cases, potentially disruptive business models to you, either as potential customers or as ecosystem partners. ARM Holdings PLC, a developer and licenser of system-on-chip semiconductors, headquartered in Cambridge, England, has had success viewing itself as the central, coordinating node of a symbiotic ecosystem of independent semiconductor manufacturers and consumer products companies, rather than as a traditional semiconductor company that develops and manufactures proprietary, standard products. Today, nearly every smartphone and mobile device includes at least one ARM design. The company achieved this ubiquity by inviting customers and consumers into its development process so that it will be the first company called by customers seeking to design a new chip. It does this in two ways: first, by incorporating knowledge across its entire ecosystem that allows it to develop optimized end-to-end solutions for customers, and second, by employing a royalty-based revenue model that ensures ARM's incentives are aligned with those of its customers.

Start new businesses by exploring the job to be done. When identifying new market opportunities, it's critical that you begin with a focus on the customer's job to be done, rather than on your company's capabilities. It's tempting to look at capabilities as the starting point for any expansion, but capabilities are of no use without a job for them. For incumbents, this requires staying focused on the job rather than on the market or capability. One example of this discipline is Corning Inc., the manufacturer of specialty glass and ceramic materials based in Corning, New York. When it becomes apparent that a Corning business can no longer generate a premium price from its technical superiority—when it reaches the efficiency innovation stage, in our framework—the company divests that business and uses the proceeds to expand businesses in the sustaining stage and to create new ones. For example, when Corning realized that liquid crystal display (LCD) would eventually replace cathode ray tube (CRT) technology to become the future of display, the company focused on the job to be done—display—rather than just on the CRT market, which at the time was important to the company. Corning began inventing products to enable the growth of the LCD industry and eventually decided to exit the CRT market.[12] To Corning, businesses serve needs, not markets, and as technological or market shifts occur, the company continues to grow by remaining focused on the need, which we call the job.

Resist the urge to force new businesses to find homes in existing units. When executives start new businesses, they often look at them and wonder, "Where do I stick this in my organization?" They feel pressure to combine new businesses with existing structures to maximize efficiency and spread overhead costs over the widest base, but this can spell doom for the new business. When a new business is housed within an existing unit, it must adopt the priorities of the existing business to secure funding; in doing so, the new business often survives in name but disappears in effect.

Once a new business is launched, it must remain independent throughout the duration of its journey, but maintaining autonomy requires ongoing leadership attention. The forces of efficiency operate 24/7 inside an organization, rooting out any cost perceived to be superfluous; standing against these forces requires the constant application of a counterforce that only the company's most senior leaders can provide. In the quest for efficiency, what has been somehow forgotten is the vital leadership role that corporate executives can play in fostering organizational innovation by countenancing the creation of multiple profit formulas and housing these different businesses in a portfolio of business models.

Use M&A to create internal business model disruption and renewal. Lastly, while we've focused most of our attention on organic activities, there's a very valuable role for M&A in a business growth engine.[13] Although at the extreme, this approach can result in a quasi-conglomerate structure that history has proved to be ineffective, there are exceptions. EMC Corp., based in Hopkinton, MA, adopted this approach with the creation of its federation structure when it floated VMware Inc., a company it had acquired three years earlier, as a publicly traded subsidiary in 2007. Much M&A activity designed to change an existing business model fails because it's done for the wrong reasons and managed in the wrong way, often resulting in the integration of units that should remain autonomous. In contrast, EMC's federation structure allows each business to pursue its individual objectives while coordinating the company's activity as a whole. This embedded capability for exploiting existing markets while identifying and investing in new markets allowed EMC to expand out of its traditional memory business into machine virtualization, agile development, and information security.

The Greatest Innovation Risk

Executives sometimes prefer to invest in their existing businesses because those investments seem less risky than trying to create entirely new businesses. But our understanding of the business model journey allows us to see that, over the long term, the greatest innovation risk a company can take is to decide *not* to create new businesses that decouple the company's future from that of its current business units.

We take great hope from the insights about business model innovation and corporate renewal that we have explored in this chapter—not because we believe that business units can evade or escape the journey that we have described, but because we believe that the corporations that house these units can. There remains much to be learned about corporate renewal and the business model journey, but we hope that insights from the business model road map can help companies learn how to create robust corporate-level business creation engines that will renew their organizations and power growth. The challenge is great—but so are the potential rewards.

Notes

1. PwC, "2015 US CEO Survey: Top Findings—Grow and Create Competitive Advantage," n.d., https://www.pwc.com/gx/en/ceo-survey/2015/assets/pwc-18th-annual-global-ceo-survey-jan-2015.pdf.

2. Z. Lindgardt and M. Ayers, "Driving Growth with Business Model Innovation," October 8, 2014, https://www.bcgperspectives.com/content/articles/growth_innovation_driving_growth_business_model_innovation.

3. See D. A. Garvin, "The Processes of Organization and Management," *MIT Sloan Management Review* 39, no. 4 (1998): 33–50. In discussing processes, we refer to all of the processes that Garvin identified in that article.

4. This business model framework was developed in 2008; see M. W. Johnson, C. M. Christensen, and H. Kagermann, "Reinventing Your Business Model," *Harvard Business Review* 86, no. 12 (2008): 50–59.

5. For more information about organizational capabilities, see C. M. Christensen and S. P. Kaufman, "Assessing Your Organization's Capabilities: Resources, Processes, and Priorities," Harvard Business School Module Note 607-014, Boston, MA, September 2006 (revised August 2008), https://www.hbs.edu/faculty/Pages/item.aspx?num=33501.

6. See E. H. Schein, *Organizational Culture and Leadership* (San Francisco, CA: Jossey-Bass, 1985).

7. It's worth noting that startups typically begin with one business unit, which is the company. Then as the organization grows, companies typically create corporate offices and business units that separate responsibility for the administration of the organization from the specific business. Today, managers tend to operate lean corporate offices that often function as thin veneers between the business and investors, but we believe that there is a vital role for the corporate office in leading business creation and developing innovation.

8. P. F. Drucker, *The Practice of Management* (New York: Harper & Row, 1954).

9. For a more complete treatment of jobs to be done, see C. M. Christensen, T. Hall, K. Dillon, and D. S. Duncan, *Competing Against Luck: The Story of Innovation and Customer Choice* (New York: HarperCollins, 2016).

10. W. Shih and M. Pierson, "Boeing 737 Industrial Footprint: The Wichita Decision," Harvard Business School Case 612-036, Boston, MA, October 2011 (revised July 2012), https://www.hbs.edu/faculty/Pages/item.aspx?num=40969.

11. S. C. Wheelwright and K. B. Clark, "Creating Project Plans to Focus Product Development," *Harvard Business Review* 70, no. 2 (1992): 70–82.

12. Authors' teleconference with David L. Morse, executive vice president and chief technology officer, Corning Inc., March 8, 2016.

13. J. Gans, *The Disruption Dilemma* (Cambridge, MA: MIT Press, 2016).

10

Managing Tensions between New and Existing Business Models

Kristian J. Sund, Marcel Bogers, J. Andrei Villarroel, and Nicolai J. Foss

Exploring new business models is a recognized way for mature companies to renew their competitive advantage. Companies explore new value propositions, deploy value propositions in new segments, change the value chain, or experiment with alternative revenue models—all in a search for a different logic for value creation and capture. Sometimes this exploration goes far beyond the existing business model and requires the creation of a new business unit. A sometimes unexpected consequence is the difficulty of fitting this new business unit into the existing organizational structure. While business model experimentation may be the raison d'être of many startup ventures, established companies typically face strong organizational rigidities that lead to tensions. Predicting these tensions and being open to experimentation with organizational structure can be the keys to a smoother business model exploration process. In this chapter, we report on a study of the European postal industry, in which we examined the organizational challenges that affect incumbent organizations in mature industries as they react to disruptive changes in their environment by seeking new business models.

Although the Romans had a type of postal service, the European postal industry as we know it today has existed for the past 500 years or so—one of the oldest, in Portugal, traces its history to 1520. For close to two centuries, established operators have been using essentially the same business model, pioneered in 1837 in the United Kingdom. In that model, senders pay a postal operator (usually through the purchase of a stamp) to bring a piece of mail or a parcel from A to B, with pricing dependent on some combination of distance, size, and weight. However, the postal industry has recently faced a rapid decline in physical mail as a result of digital substitution, while regulatory liberalization has boosted the level of competition in postal markets. Many postal operators have reacted by exploring new opportunities in the digital marketplace.

By interviewing managers and reviewing relevant information, we studied Danish, Portuguese, and Swiss postal operators to find out how they have dealt with the challenge of exploring new business models since the turn of the millennium. The organizations we studied strived to maintain their core business while at the same time incubating new ventures. Managers at all of the organizations felt there were potential new business models that they could benefit from developing, but when exploring the building blocks of these business models, they found that tensions emerged in their organizations. It required a separate process of organizational experimentation to find out how to organize for business model exploration.

Managing the Tensions

Our research points to three key areas of tension almost any existing business will face if it attempts to discover entirely new business models. Whether management succeeds in handling those tensions will determine their success in identifying and implementing new business models.

Don't settle too quickly on structure. Top management is typically trained to see organizational structure as a means of executing strategy. As the business historian Alfred D. Chandler put it, "structure follows strategy." In the case of business model exploration, however, our research suggests it's a mistake for management to settle too quickly on a strategy and structure for the new business. In 2006, the Danish postal service, Post Danmark A/S, acquired Strålfors, an information logistics company, and subsequently positioned some of the company's other innovative ventures within this subsidiary. It was thought there were possible synergies in merging products, but the fit was less than perfect, and as one manager put it, ultimately the business units "moved a bit around over the years." The Danish and Swedish posts subsequently merged to form a new company, now called PostNord AB. PostNord at one point signaled to the market that Strålfors was for sale but then, in the fall of 2015, announced that it would retain ownership of Strålfors, after all. A manager from another postal operator offered a similar account of the struggle with how to fit a new venture into an old company, pointing out how that operator had to "constantly learn and modify ... how we organize ourselves."

The lesson for any organization wanting to explore new business models is to not settle too quickly on a structure for the new business. In fact, the organizational structure can more usefully be thought of as one of the essential building blocks of the business model—that is, as an aspect of the new business that needs to be fully explored and experimented with before you can learn what works best.

Balance top management support and experimentation. Exploring new business models is a strategic decision aimed at adapting the company's activities to an evolving business landscape and discovering new revenue streams. At the postal operators we studied, this involved numerous initiatives. For example, the Swiss Post decided there might be an opportunity to expand its partnerships with online retail businesses beyond picking up and delivering parcels. The Swiss Post could leverage its established, trusted brand by selling secure sockets layer (SSL) certificates, digital signature solutions, and email certificates to online retailers and other businesses. However, setting up the new business unit involved the creation of new capabilities, both on the IT and the sales sides. It was recognized that this new business unit would be very different from the organization's existing core business. The solution involved acquiring a startup that had developed some core solutions in this space and then building the business with a mix of management and staff hired from outside as well as transferred from the core business.

Management clearly identified a need to protect the fledgling business from above. The new business unit was a strategic initiative and as such needed to be shepherded by top management. As one manager told us, "We really managed to make sure that from the top ... these organizations were protected. You need to have ownership by the CEO; otherwise, this is destroyed extremely quickly." However, it was also gradually recognized that top management should not try to steer the new business unit. As one manager said, "It is clearly an advantage if people [in the new business unit] are a little bit remote of the headquarters.

The headquarters has an existing way of doing business ... you develop much more successfully if you give these people space and distance to the core." This implies a balancing act for top management between protecting and coaching, on the one hand, and leaving the new business unit to experiment, on the other.

Expect a power struggle for resources. Any new business model has to grow and coexist with existing business models that may be stagnating but still provide the lion's share of revenues for the company. Managers of such existing business models can be powerful and may have turf to protect in the internal struggle for resources. They and their employees may feel threatened if the new business unit becomes too successful. Furthermore, the new business model may not be profitable for a long time, leading to the risk that needed investments are diverted from more profitable parts of the business. One manager told us that this "has perhaps been the biggest barrier—that we are competing and working to get access to the same IT resources within the company."

Top management needs to manage this potential competition for resources between the new business and the old core business. One way to achieve this is to accept multiple business logics, as well as multiple performance management and measurement systems. As one manager explained, "We quite successfully managed to convince the internal management that, for the moment, revenue streams shall not be the most important performance indicator." Alternative metrics could include the estimated market potential, for example.

A point to consider is the importance of communicating across the company why it is engaging in business model exploration and how this will benefit the company in the long term. Conflicts for scarce resources within the organization cannot be avoided completely, but they can be softened if employees across business units build a shared understanding of the objectives of the business model exploration.

The Organizational Dimension

The business model canvas framework developed by Alexander Osterwalder and Yves Pigneur has become a very popular way to understand the potential building blocks of business models. The canvas highlights nine such building blocks: customer segments, value propositions, channels, customer relationships, revenue streams, key resources, key activities, key partnerships, and cost structure. However, organizational designs and the associated organizational tensions that emerge during the process of business model exploration are not well addressed by the existing tools. Companies exploring new business models may not fully recognize that these tensions will almost inevitably emerge and thus may be ill prepared to manage them. Understanding these tensions should help in managing the challenges of concurrent business models.

The tensions we highlight imply that the design of an organizational structure that accommodates both new and older business models needs to be considered an intricate part of business model innovation. Organizational design has to be questioned and experimented with as part of the exploration. A top management team that is prepared for such exploration and aware of the organizational dimension of business model exploration may well be more likely to succeed at business model innovation.

Related Research

M. Bogers, K. J. Sund, and J. A. Villarroel, "The Organizational Dimension of Business Model Exploration: Evidence from the European Postal Industry," in *Business Model Innovation: The Organizational Dimension*, ed. Nicolai J. Foss and Tina Saebi, 269–287 (Oxford: Oxford University Press, 2015).

11

Why Great New Products Fail

Duncan Simester

A lot of great new products fail—and companies often wonder why. Although the companies were careful to listen to their customers, the products still failed. This is not a rare occurrence. A recent study of almost 9,000 new products that achieved broad distribution at a national retailer revealed that just 40% of them were still sold three years later.[1]

About the Research

This article was motivated by a paradox: Most companies are now diligent about listening to their customers, yet their new products still fail. This paradox contrasts two observations: (1) many companies engage customers in the new product development process, but (2) many new products still fail. Evidence of the first point is readily apparent when speaking to companies about their product development process. However, the rate of new product failures is a difficult statistic to calculate. Although successes are easily identified, failures are much more difficult to account for. The statistic reported in the first paragraph of this article uses data from a very large US retailer that my research team has conducted research with over the last 10 years. We can see new products entering the retailer's stores and observe how many of them are still being sold three years later.[2] This provides an accurate measure of how many of this retailer's new products failed. However, even this number almost certainly understates the overall new product failure rate. Achieving distribution on the shelves of this retailer is itself an achievement. If we were able to measure the thousands of new products that failed to gain shelf space, the overall failure rate would be considerably higher.

Having first identified the paradox, the article then identifies a resolution: While businesses are diligent in designing great products, they often ignore how customers learn which products are great. As a result, great products fail because customers do not know they are great. This explanation was distilled from a review of academic research studying how customers make purchasing decisions. Fundamental academic research on this topic is deep and interdisciplinary, extending from social psychology to signaling theory (a branch of theoretical economics). Much of the research is technical, and the findings are widely dispersed. As a result, the findings are poorly understood by executives. The purpose of this article is to survey this broad technical body of knowledge and summarize the findings into key insights that describe when customers will recognize that new products are great, and when greatness will be overlooked. The central pillars of this framework are (1) customer search and (2) customer inference. If businesses can understand when customers will search and when they will form inferences, they can better predict when customers will embrace their innovations and when they will ignore them.

Some of these products did not create value for customers and deserved to fail. However, many would have created value if customers had adopted them. But customers could not, or did not, recognize their value.

While most companies focus on customer needs, they do not think hard enough about how customers decide what to purchase. We now have ample insight into how customers evaluate new products. Yet companies generally focus primarily on creating value—without enough regard to whether customers will recognize this value.

To decide what to buy, customers need to know what products are available and how their features vary. Whether you are

an airline choosing which aircraft to purchase, a college gradu-
ate choosing your first car, or a parent buying diapers for your
infant, there are only two ways you can collect this information.
You can search, or you can infer. The inference process uses the
information you can search for to guess the information that
you cannot easily search for. We will start by discussing the
search process before turning to the inference process.

Customers' Search Process

In July 2012, United Airlines Inc. announced a large commercial aircraft purchase, with an agreement to purchase 150 Boeing
737 aircraft for $14.7 billion. The deal took a year just to negoti-
ate, and before that, the team from United engaged in extensive
research trying to understand the capabilities of different aircraft
and the costs of operating and servicing them.[3] Imposing structure and discipline on this search process is one of the primary
roles of a procurement department. The length and intensity of
the search process is a function of its cost, the importance of the
decision, and the customer's expertise.

For a customer, the perceived benefit of searching for a better
solution may not be the same as the actual benefit, particularly
in markets with little recent innovation. This poses a challenge
for significant innovations in such markets; customers may not
find these innovations because they do not know to look. For
example, when British shower manufacturer Aqualisa Products
Ltd. developed an innovative new shower system for the UK
residential market, customers did not initially adopt the product
because they were accustomed to the UK's low water pressure,
which this product addressed. Customers did not realize that a

better shower system was possible and therefore saw no reason to look for one.[4]

In other situations, the benefits of information are clear, but the cost of searching for it is simply too high. For example, when flying into New York City's La Guardia Airport, many of us will use a yellow taxi to get to Manhattan. In 2014, there were more taxi accidents in New York City than there were taxi medallions.[5] The implication: It is important to find a safe taxi driver. But what do we do when exiting the terminal carrying our luggage? Most of us jump into the first cab in the line. Although the benefits of finding a safe taxi driver are clear, the cost of searching for it is simply too high—particularly in settings where passengers are encouraged to just take the next available taxi. One suggestion: Walk around the taxi before you get in and see if there are any big dents, particularly around the passenger compartment.

The relationship between how much customers search and their prior expertise is surprising. In an influential study using data of new car purchases, researchers Sridhar Moorthy, Brian Ratchford, and Debabrata Talukdar showed that the relationship can be an inverted U.[6]

Customers with a lot of expertise (experts) may not search, because they think they already know what's best. For example, a pharmaceutical company was recently surprised when doctors did not prescribe its new drug. The drug was a fabulous new product that created tremendous value for customers: It treated the disease more effectively and had fewer side effects than existing treatments. However, it was the first innovation in this therapeutic area for many years. Doctors believed that they already knew all there was to be known about how to treat the disease, and so their minds were not open to the possibility of new treatments.

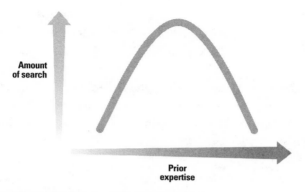

The Relationship between Expertise and Search

Research suggests that there can be a surprising relationship between the amount of prior expertise a consumer has about a product category and the extent to which he or she searches for information before making a purchase decision. Customers with a lot of expertise may not search, because they think they already know what's best, and customers who know very little about the category may not know where to begin.

At the other end of this spectrum are customers who are clueless. They do not search because they do not know which questions to ask, where to find the answers, or how to interpret the information if it arrives. For instance, I once had a friend call on a Saturday morning and ask for help buying a bicycle. Fine plan (when you are clueless ask for help), but poor execution (I knew nothing about bikes). Not wanting to disappoint my friend, I accompanied her to the bike store, where we explained that she needed a bike, and I was there to help with her decision. The enthusiastic young salesman started describing the technical differences between the bikes. This went on for 20 minutes until my friend's eyes were completely glazed over. She stopped the salesman, looked him in the eye, and said, "I want a red bike."

The salesman responded, "Well, I better take you to the red bike section then." We walked out 10 minutes later with a red bike. Think for a moment about the implications of this example for a bike manufacturer. Technical innovation would not increase the chances of a sale to this customer, no matter how much value the innovations created. More generally, the risk for companies is that they invest in innovations that customers cannot recognize.

Consumers' Inference Process

When search is incomplete, we shift to forming inferences; we use what we can observe to infer what is too costly or too difficult to search for. We have already seen one example of a cue that customers can use to form inferences: using dents in taxis to infer the quality of the driver. McDonald's Corp. offers another illustration. The fast-food chain has long emphasized to franchisees the importance of keeping a restaurant's parking area clean.[7] Why, you might wonder? Customers do not really care about the parking area. What they care about is the cleanliness of the kitchen, and perhaps the bathrooms. But what can customers see when they drive past? They may use the cleanliness of the parking area (what they can see) to infer the cleanliness of the kitchen and bathrooms (what they care about). What is most surprising is that when you ask customers why they did not choose to stop, they often cannot tell you; they just did not feel comfortable stopping at that restaurant. In other words, this is not a conscious thought process; it is operating at the subconscious level, which makes it both pervasive and powerful.

We can illustrate this principle through a visual example created by vision science professor Edward H. Adelson.[8] On the left

The Checker Shadow Illusion

When we look at the checkerboard image, our eyes are leading us to inferences; we do not know that it is happening, and even if we did, we could not do anything about it. Although purchasing decisions are a different neural process than this visual process, a similar phenomenon occurs when customers are evaluating different products or services: Customers often do not realize they are forming inferences, and even if they do, they are powerless to stop it.

is a checkerboard, with a black square labeled "A" and an apparently white square labeled "B." In fact, squares A and B are both the same shade of gray. We demonstrate this on the right, where we have removed the surrounding context. Even more remarkable, now that you know this is true, look back to the left and try to tell your eyes that the A and B squares are the same color. You can't. Our eyes are leading us to inferences; we do not know that it is happening, and even if we did, we could not do anything about it.[9] Although purchasing decisions are a different neural process than this visual process, a similar phenomenon occurs when customers are evaluating different products or services. Customers often do not realize they are forming inferences, and even if they do, they are powerless to stop it.

The Role of the Brand

The most common cues we use to infer product quality are price and brand. In a business-to-business setting, signaling information about quality is essentially the only role of the brand. Even in consumer markets, this signaling role is hugely important.[10] However, in some consumer markets, brands may signal more than just product quality; consumers can also use brands to signal information about themselves.[11]

In many circumstances, the more effectively customers can search, the less they will rely on the brand. Moreover, their perceptions of the brand will change quickly as new information comes in. Both factors diminish the importance of the brand. However, in markets where customers cannot search easily and effectively, they are forced to use the brand to make purchasing decisions. For example, if customers want to buy a reliable laptop computer with state-of-the-art features, they have two options. If they are knowledgeable, they can search computers' spec sheets and reviews to evaluate the computers' features. Alternatively, they can form an inference based upon the computer brand. For customers who lack the expertise to evaluate computers' features, relying on the brand may be the only option.

In general, customers prefer to search. It is usually only when they are unable to search effectively, either because they lack expertise or because the cost is too high, that they rely upon the brand. Second, the role of the brand may vary across customers. A novice computer buyer may lack the expertise to search and be forced to rely upon inference. Most computer buyers have enough expertise to simply engage in search.

Similarly, we can expect the brand to play a more prominent role for prospective customers than for existing customers. This became apparent to a consulting firm that was innovating in its consulting processes. In a professional services setting, as in any services setting, there is generally no spec sheet, and prospective customers are often forced to rely on inference. As a result, the firm's prospective customers are unlikely to reward it for its process improvements, although they may infer the quality of the firm based on the strength of its brand. This contrasts with the firm's existing customers, who experience the process improvements firsthand.

Third, the role of the brand may vary across product features. Features that are on the spec sheet, such as the size of a laptop's hard drive, are typically features than can be discovered through search. However, features that do not appear on the spec sheet, such as reliability or ease of use, are not easily discovered through search (although reviews from trusted sources can be helpful), and thus it is these features for which the brand's role will be more prominent.

The Impact of the Internet

How has the internet affected the role of the brand and the way that customers make purchasing decisions? We should first recognize that for some products, or at least some product features, the internet has had relatively little impact on how customers make purchasing decisions. For example, the internet does not help us search for information about future events, such as how Volkswagen AG will respond to future product recalls, or how well security software will protect against the next generation of online threats. It is also less helpful for product attributes that require physical inspection, particularly when the needs are specific to the user (such as the fit and appearance of a swimsuit).[12]

The internet has had a profound impact on the way that customers evaluate many other products, however. It has done so in two ways. First, it has lowered the cost of search by making information more accessible.[13] The initial impact of this change was perhaps smaller than anticipated in some markets. When customers shop in physical stores, they do not have ready access to a laptop or desktop computer. It was not until the advent of smartphones that the internet substantially lowered the cost of search in many markets.

The second impact of the internet has been to broaden the number of product features that are searchable. User-generated content, including blogs and product reviews, now mean that customers can search for information about features that were previously unsearchable, such as the quality of a golf course or the fairness of a contractor.

Consider how this has changed the restaurant market. It used to be that tourists in a new city had little choice but to ask the hotel concierge for a recommendation or choose a restaurant that had a big national brand. This was a good outcome for chains, including the Hard Rock Café. How do tourists make restaurant choices now? They pick up their smartphone and query TripAdvisor.com or Yelp.com. They can compare prices, menus, location, even how politely they will be greeted by the *maître d'*. This has sharply diminished the role of the brand. Now small, innovative restaurants offering great food and service become easier to discover, while the Hard Rock Café has closed some of its locations.[14]

Does this mean that the internet has increased or decreased price competition? If customers can now recognize greatness where they previously could not, companies with innovative products will benefit, as customers will pay a larger premium for those products. On the other hand, in cases where customers were paying a premium for differentiation that was perceived rather than actual, the internet will foster competition and undermine that premium.[15] For example, if a viral video revealed that national brand and private-label vitamins are identical products made in the same factory, some consumers would probably stop paying a premium for the national brands.

What Should Companies Do Differently?

For companies engaged in innovation or product development, the implications are clear: They need to ensure not just that they create products that create value for customers but also that customers can recognize this value. We recommend that companies focus on three sets of questions.

First, are customers *motivated to search*? Do they recognize that there could be a better solution, and are they willing to invest effort to find that solution? Recall the Aqualisa example: Because customers did not know a better shower was possible, they were not motivated to look for it. How much does the solution differ from existing options? If this is the first major innovation in the industry for 20 years, customers are less likely to be searching for new alternatives than if the industry has had a steady stream of major innovations. A concrete measure of how motivated customers are to search is the length of their procurement or decision process. For example, customers on average

Will Customers Discover Your Innovation?

If customers do not discover your innovations, they will not increase your sales. The following questions can help you assess how likely customers are to discover your innovative new product or service.

Motivation to Search	• Do customers recognize the need as important? • Do they think they already have a solution? • How different is your solution from what's been available? • How long is the typical customer's decision process?
Ability to Search	• How difficult is it to search? • Is the improvement measured on a spec sheet or its equivalent? • Can customers interpret the information? • Will they have to change their search process?
Customer Inferences	• What cues do customers use to make inferences? • What will they infer from these cues? • Can you control or influence these cues?

spend 15 to 20 hours searching for information when buying a new car.[16] However, few customers will invest this amount of time when choosing detergent for their dishes.

Second, are customers *able to search effectively*? Traditionally, the litmus test for this question was whether the information was listed on a spec sheet. Recall the laptop computer example: The size of the hard drive is on the spec sheet and searchable, but the reliability and ease of use are not. As long as customers have the expertise to interpret the spec sheet, features on the spec sheet are generally searchable. If the decision is important enough but customers lack expertise, they may still be able to search by turning to expert advisers. Examples of expert advisers include doctors, financial advisers, real estate agents, insurance brokers, IT consultants, and workplace benefits consultants. In some markets, customers can use customer reviews to search for information that is not on the spec sheet. In this case, the spec sheet is no longer as good a litmus test of whether customers are likely to search rather than infer. One factor that has not changed: Customers typically adopt a decision process, and changing this decision process is difficult. For example, if customers have always searched for the best deals on cars by waiting until the end of the model year, then convincing them to purchase earlier in the model year will be difficult.

If customers cannot search, companies need to understand *what cues they will use* to infer the absent information. It is an indication of how well McDonald's manages its restaurants that it knows not just that customers infer restaurant cleanliness from the state of the parking lots but also that customers do this subconsciously. You may have to create cues to help customers with this inference process. For example, automobile manufacturers would like to convince customers that the engines and transmissions in their cars are precisely engineered. Because the quality of the engineering of these components is not observable to customers, car companies instead highlight engineering features that are observable. Recall the car advertisements in which ball bearings roll along door seams. Most customers don't really care how precisely ball bearings track on their car's door seams. However, the manufacturer has provided a cue to infer the quality of its engineering. Customers can use this cue to evaluate the engineering of parts that they cannot observe or do not have the expertise to evaluate.

Developing great products is not enough to succeed in business — companies have to develop great products that customers can recognize as great.

Helping Customers Recognize Innovation

Developing great products is not enough to succeed in business—companies have to develop great products that customers can recognize as great. Fortunately, the way that customers collect information and make purchasing decisions is now understood. Rather than merely asking what customers need, companies have to understand how customers will evaluate which products will satisfy their needs.

If customers are motivated to learn about products and have the expertise to interpret what they learn, then we can expect the search process to play an important role in their decisions. This is a welcome situation for innovative companies, as customers are more likely to recognize their innovations. However, when customers are either not sufficiently motivated or not sufficiently informed, then search will give way to inference. This makes it much less likely that customers will recognize innovations. The implications for companies are clear: Focus development on innovations that your customers will easily recognize, or find ways to alert them to innovations they may not detect on their own.

Notes

1. E. Anderson, S. Lin, D. Simester, and C. Tucker, "Harbingers of Failure," *Journal of Marketing Research* 52, no. 5 (2015): 580–592.

2. Anderson et al., "Harbingers of Failure."

3. C. Isidore, "Boeing Wins $14.7 Billion Jet Order from United," July 12, 2012, http://money.cnn.com/2012/07/12/news/companies/boeing-united/index.htm.

4. Y. E. Moon and K. Herman, "Aqualisa Quartz: Simply a Better Shower," Harvard Business School Case 502-030, Boston, MA, January 2002 (revised July 2006), https://www.hbs.edu/faculty/Pages/item.aspx?num=28768.

5. See L. P. Banville, "Taxi Cab Accidents in New York: 1999–2014," December 10, 2014, https://banvillelaw.com/taxi-cab-accidents-new-york-1999-2014; and New York City Taxi & Limousine Commission, "2014 Taxi Cab Fact Book," http://www.nyc.gov/html/tlc/downloads/pdf/2014_taxicab_fact_book.pdf.

6. S. Moorthy, B. T. Ratchford, and D. Talukdar, "Consumer Information Search Revisited: Theory and Empirical Analysis," *Journal of Consumer Research* 23, no. 4 (1997): 263–277.

7. J. Pepin, "Burger Meister Ray Kroc," *Time*, December 7, 1998.

8. See E. H. Adelson, "Checkershadow Illusion," 1995, http://persci.mit.edu/gallery/checkershadow.

9. For another surprising example of these visual effects, see R. B. Lotto and D. Purves, "The Effects of Color on Brightness," *Nature Neuroscience* 2, no. 11 (1999): 1010–1014.

10. Prominent studies of the signaling role of the brand include T. Erdem and J. Swait, "Brand Equity as a Signaling Phenomenon," *Journal of Consumer Psychology* 7, no. 2 (1998): 131–157; and B. Wernerfelt, "Umbrella Branding as a Signal of New Product Quality: An Example of Signaling by Posting a Bond," *Rand Journal of Economics* 19, no. 3 (1988): 458–466.

11. This second signaling role of the brand is particularly important if consumption is conspicuous. For example, when we wear a Rolex watch, drive a BMW vehicle, carry a Louis Vuitton bag, or talk on an iPhone, our consumption is conspicuous to others. In these settings, consumers may enlist brands to convey signals about themselves. Wearing a Rolex watch signals success and perhaps good taste—personal characteristics that are desirable to communicate, but objectionable to mention explicitly. See Y. J. Han, J. C. Nunes, and X. Drèze, "Signaling Status with Luxury Goods: The Role of Brand Prominence," *Journal of Marketing* 74, no. 4 (2010): 15–30.

12. Rajiv Lal and Miklos Sarvary draw a distinction between what they term *digital attributes*, which can be searched online, and *nondigital attributes*, which cannot. See R. Lal and M. Sarvary, "When and How Is the Internet Likely to Decrease Price Competition," *Marketing Science* 18, no. 4 (1999): 485–503.

13. F. Zettelmeyer, F. S. Morton, and J. Silva-Risso, "How the Internet Lowers Prices: Evidence from Matched Survey and Automobile Transaction Data," *Journal of Marketing Research* 43, no. 2 (2006): 168–181.

14. C. Tice, "Hard Rock Café Hits Some Sour Notes But Keeps Rolling," March 2, 2010, https://www.cbsnews.com/news/hard-rock-cafe-hits-some-sour-notes-but-keeps-rolling.

15. John G. Lynch Jr. and Dan Ariely demonstrated this point in a clever study of wine markets. They found that making it easier to obtain information about quality reduces price sensitivity for differentiated wines. However, when the internet revealed that the wines were undifferentiated, price sensitivity among customers increased. See J. G. Lynch Jr. and D. Ariely, "Wine Online: Search Costs Affect Competition on Price, Quality, and Distribution," *Marketing Science* 19, no. 1 (2000): 83–103.

16. B. Ratchford, D. Talukdar, and M. S. Lee, "The Impact of the Internet on Consumers' Use of Information Sources for Automobiles: A Re-Inquiry," *Journal of Consumer Research* 34, no. 1 (2007): 111–119.

12

Creating Better Innovation Measurement Practices

Anders Richtnér, Anna Brattström, Johan Frishammar, Jennie Björk, and Mats Magnusson

For most companies, innovation is a top managerial priority. Many managers look at successful innovators such as Apple Inc. and Google Inc. with envy, wishing their companies could be half as innovative. To boost and benchmark innovation, managers often use quantitative performance indicators.[1] Some of these indicators measure innovation as *results* or *outcomes* such as sales from new products. Others measure innovation as a *process*, using metrics such as the number of innovation projects in progress. And some track *input* measures such as the number of ideas generated, while still others focus on the *innovation portfolio*, by looking at factors such as the percentage of investments in breakthrough projects versus product line extensions.

Our research on innovation measurement suggests that the key managerial challenge is not identifying metrics—there is no shortage of measures to choose from. Nor should the goal be to find the perfect metric, since that quest is often futile. Rather, the crux of effective innovation measurement is to understand the problem that measurement should solve for the organization and, based on that insight, to design and implement a useful and usable innovation measurement framework appropriate to the organization's needs.

In this process, identifying the right questions is usually more difficult than finding the appropriate answers. Executives need to understand the innovation challenges the company faces, how innovation is currently measured, and the extent to which current measurement practices help or hinder efforts to achieve the organization's innovation goals. Only then will managers be able to steer clear of common innovation measurement mistakes.

Some of the most insidious mistakes involve placing too much value on data at the expense of meaning and getting bogged down with too many measures that provide contradictory advice and incentivize employees to do the wrong things. Although companies use performance measurement for almost any activity, measurement of innovation is by no means straightforward.

Managers often get hung up on selecting and implementing the appropriate measures. The goal of this article is to help managers ask the right questions about how to measure innovation and translate their insights into effective innovation measurement practices. We have developed a practical, step-by-step framework that helps managers identify *whether* their current innovation measurement practices need to change and, if so, *how* to go about measuring innovation more effectively. The framework is also aimed at companies that do not currently apply metrics systematically to innovation but would like to start.

Our framework is grounded in both innovation measurement literature and our research, which included a survey of managers as well as case studies of three global, innovation-intensive companies (a consumer goods company, a mining company, and a manufacturer of machinery).

About the Research

In our research, which spanned more than three years, we explicitly sought to move beyond a focus on *what* aspects of the innovation process to measure to understanding *whether* companies' current innovation measurement practices need to change and *how* to go about measuring innovation more effectively. Our data was collected in four phases.

First, we distributed a survey with open-ended questions (for example, managers were asked to write short essays) to 45 managers from 21 companies; all of the managers surveyed were involved in the measurement of innovation. We also conducted three expert interviews within a consulting firm that specializes in innovation management and measurement. Based on these inputs, we identified a set of mistakes, challenges, and issues pertaining to the measurement of innovation.

Second, we worked closely with three large companies: a consumer goods company, a mining company, and a machine products company. At those companies, we collected data from interviews, documents, meetings, and workshops. This generated a comprehensive analysis of the innovation measurement practices in these companies. Although the companies are active in different industries, we were able to identify commonalities in their practices. Based on data gathered in these first two steps, we developed a draft of our paper and process model.

Third, we conducted feedback interviews using our emergent findings. The interviewees confirmed to us that our general interpretations and conclusions were reasonable, while also providing additional insights that allowed us to substantiate and fine tune our framework.

Fourth, we conducted five additional workshops, attended by more than 80 managers from more than 50 organizations. At these workshops, we described the traps and the process model and asked for feedback and verification. The workshops convinced us that our findings were relevant to a broad set of companies from a range of industries.

Our research allowed us to identify common mistakes, issues, and challenges associated with the measurement of innovation. Based on these insights, we developed our framework, which we verified and tested with additional interviews and workshops that included managers from more than 50 companies.

Three Common Traps

Most of the companies that took part in our research reported
that they measure their innovation activities. However, they
said their measurement efforts often failed to generate desired
results. The root causes became clear in our initial analysis.
For example, many companies used quantitative measures but
neglected to use qualitative measures (such as employees' skill
level or the freedom employees have to explore fields outside the
core business). Others overemphasized short-term measures over
long-term measures, because they viewed short-term measures
as more convenient. Some of the underlying issues, however,
were less obvious and led to measurement activities that triggered unintended, unforeseen, unpleasant, or negative effects
that were difficult to overcome or avoid.[2,3] What emerged from
our research were three important innovation measurement
traps to avoid: (1) overestimating or underestimating the potential of innovation measurement, (2) measuring only the parts as
opposed to the whole, and (3) overlooking the political power of
innovation measures.

**Trap 1: Overestimating or Underestimating What Innovation
Measurement Can Do**

Some of the companies we studied were too detailed in the way
they measured innovation; they assumed that once things were
measured they could be managed. Other companies did practi-
cally no measurement at all, on the assumption that measuring innovation was inherently counterproductive and harmful
to creativity and novelty. Companies in the first group overestimated what innovation measurement could do; those in the
second group underestimated it.

Comprehensive measurement of innovation allows managers to follow up on inputs, the innovation process itself, and its outcomes. However, excessively detailed measurement of everything harms innovation outcomes. As the saying goes, not everything that can be counted counts, and not everything that counts can be counted.

One company that overestimated what measurement can do was a global consumer goods company that does business in more than 100 countries. It added a wide array of innovation measures to ensure better management and optimize resource allocation. However, the measures it selected discouraged radical innovation, and the implementation resulted in information overflow, burdensome administration, and decision-making delays. Toward the end of our study, management realized it was on the wrong track and began to revise its innovation measurement practices.

Another company we studied that systematically underestimated the value of innovation measurement is consistently listed as one of the world's top five players in the mining industry. The company's management was highly skeptical of innovation measurement, and as a result it hardly measured innovation at all. This made follow-up and management of innovation inherently difficult. At the end of our study, this company initiated a process of revamping its innovation measures and innovation-related activities.

Trap 2: Measuring Parts but Not the Whole

In the companies we studied, managerial attention was often directed to individual bits and pieces of the innovation process. Executives frequently failed to formulate a holistic overview of innovation inputs, activities, and outputs, or they focused too specifically on individual projects at the expense of their overall innovation portfolio.

The mining company, for example, made the mistake of frequently running similar projects in parallel. This prevented managers from focusing on the most pressing issues. It also disrupted the flow of the innovation process, created bottlenecks, and resulted in a growing frustration among both engineers and managers. What's more, it harmed efforts to allocate innovation resources effectively. As one manager told us, "It is unclear who is actually entitled to start a new innovation project at our company and who has the overall responsibility for the portfolio of projects."

In another example, a few years ago, when a large global manufacturer of heavy vehicles implemented measures to track the innovation process, front-load problem solving, and ensure innovation projects were sufficiently resourced, it discovered that it had overlooked two important elements: measurement of innovation outputs and measurement of market preconditions for innovation. Although managers had a clear overview of what went into the process and how it proceeded, they could not follow up on innovation outputs or determine whether their innovation efforts were attuned with prevailing market conditions. In response, the company revised its innovation measures, adding new measures to reflect market conditions and how innovative projects were, plus a quarterly plan for when each project was expected to reach the market. The changes allow the company to better prioritize its innovation activities without diluting its overall innovative efforts.

Trap 3: Overlooking the Political Aspect of Innovation Measures

Any manager who wants to create or revise innovation measurement practices needs to understand the political implications of making changes. In most organizations, what gets measured is what gets done, and what gets done is what gets rewarded. Changing the way innovation gets measured therefore implies that some groups or goals will become more important while others will become less important. In the companies we studied, there were often heated discussions about what to measure, when, and why. Although such discussions can be fruitful, they can also be harmful, particularly if members of the organization remain unsure about what to focus on.

For example, at the consumer goods company mentioned earlier, the research and development (R&D) department's innovation-related activities had historically been well funded. Unfortunately, the investments did not result in sufficient insights about customer needs. As one manager commented, "The R&D department took ages to develop the 'perfect product'—but it wasn't perfect because the market didn't want it."

The company attempted to make changes in measurement to overcome this problem but encountered fierce resistance, particularly from R&D. "It took about a year to get everyone on board and understanding our new ways of following up and tracking innovation," one manager recalled. To overcome resistance and political struggles, management initiated a cross-functional initiative to look at innovation measurement.

Enhancing Innovation Measurement Practices

We encourage managers to recognize the three potential traps
we have described before getting serious about creating new
innovation measurement practices or revising existing ones.
In our view, the biggest challenge is not identifying the right
set of measures for a company but understanding the various
blind spots that companies can encounter in determining how
to measure innovation.

Mindful of the three traps, how can companies best implement new or revised innovation metrics? Drawing on our
research, we have defined a three-phase process that can help
companies improve their innovation management practices: (A)
assess current innovation measurement practices, (B) *improve*
core innovation measurement practices, and (C) *deploy* the
improved innovation measurement practices.

Each phase involves distinct activities that companies should
go through and includes questions to consider. The three phases
unfold iteratively, where changes in one phase trigger adapta-
tions in others. In the following section, we describe the three
stages and the seven steps that comprise them, in detail.

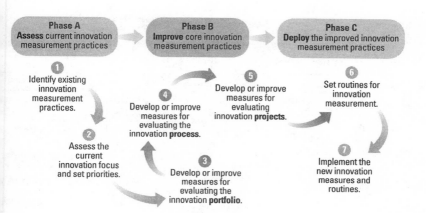

A Framework for Improving Innovation Measurement

Companies can develop more effective innovation management practices in three phases: (1) assessing current innovation measurement practices, (2) improving those core innovation measurement practices, and (3) deploying the improved metrics.

Implementing the Innovation Measurement Framework

Companies that are changing their innovation measurement practices need to conside a number of key questions during each step of the process.

Phases	Steps	Actions and questions to consider		
Phase A: Assess current innovation measurement practices	1. Identify existing innovation measurement practices.	Compile a list of all key measures and measurement activities in your organization.		
		• Can you identify particular patterns? • Are you using qualitative or quantitative measures, or both? • What is the frequency of follow-up?	• Which tools and routines for innovation measurement are currently applied? • Which of your measures have a direct effect on innovation— and which have an indirect effect?	• Who uses the key innovation measures, when, and for what purpose? • How are key innovation measures linked to incentive systems?
	2. Assess the current innovation focus and set priorities.	Assess your innovation goals and priorities.		
		What's the desired balance between serving existing customers versus entering new markets versus targeting new customer needs?		Where is your core innovation focus? Products, services, business model, technology or process, or a combination of these?

Phase B: Improve core innovation measurement practices	3. Develop or improve measures for evaluating the innovation portfolio.	Develop measures that help you assess what type of innovation initiatives are underway and how far they are from realization.		
		To what extent do you make explicit strategic choices in the balancing of the portfolio?	Are you discovering and evaluating the balance between high- and low-risk projects; large and small projects; and radical and incremental innovation projects?	
		Consider using the following measures:		
		Proportion of innovation resources/projects devoted to incremental, extension, and breakthrough initiatives in the short and long term	Percentage of projects targeted to result in offerings that are new or in new markets	ROI for new products or services
	4. Develop or improve measures for evaluating the innovation process.	Develop measures that help you focus on what is important to you: speed, resource consumption, and/or output.		
		Have you identified measures of input, throughput, and output for the innovation process?		
		Consider using the following measures:		
		• Percentage of projects launched that lead to revenue • Average duration of the innovation process versus target performance • Average project performance against schedule/target	• Number and percentage of projects in different stages in the innovation process • Number and percentage of projects terminated after each stage • Number of projects stalled	

5. Develop or improve measures for evaluating innovation projects.	Develop measures that help you spot bottlenecks in innovation projects and help make the projects customer-centric.		
	Do you know why projects stand still?	Is there enough slack for innovation?	Are mechanisms for securing external feedback an integral part of projects?
	Consider using the following measures:		
	• Percentage of time project is moving ahead versus waiting for input or resources • Number of prototypes per new product/service • Number of customer tests before launch	• Number of patent applications • Time from idea submission to commercial launch • Time to profitability • Project cost versus budget • Percentage of projects involving third parties	

Phase C: Deploy the improved innovation measurement practices	6. Set routines for innovation measurement.	Set up targets and follow-up activities.	
		• Decide the appropriate total number of innovation measures. • Decide which measures can change over time, and which should be kept constant. • Decide how innovation measures should be linked to general performance assessment and incentive systems.	• Set targets for each of the measures identified in Phase B. • Decide the frequency of measurement. • Assign a responsible "owner" for each measure or group of measures.
	7. Implement the new innovation measures and routines.	Make sure the new innovation measures are being used.	
		Make a reasonable time plan for implementing the new innovation measurement practices.	Ensure commitment to new innovation measurements from key stakeholders.	Ensure that new innovation measurement practices are known within the organization.

Phase A: Assess Current Innovation Measurement Practices

A key to successful change is to start by thoroughly mapping the current situation to assess current practices for measuring innovation. Carefully discussing and agreeing upon innovation measurement practices and the current innovation focus can enable more careful follow-up and prioritization of activities while avoiding dead ends and unproductive activities that produce data without meaning. This, in turn, helps executives avoid the first trap we identified in our research: measuring too much or too little.

Important questions to answer in this phase include:

- Do your current innovation measurement practices help or hurt your ability to achieve your innovation goals and priorities?
- To what extent are the current practices aligned with the overall company strategy?

Step 1: Identify existing innovation measurement practices.
Most companies currently measure innovation performance somehow. But we found the usefulness of measures varies across companies. As one manager at a global consumer goods company told us, "We measure innovation, but we don't have perfect key performance indicators."

The first fundamental step toward improving innovation measurement is to identify and make explicit the number of innovation measures that are already in use. Putting them all on the table provides an overview and allows them to be categorized. The outcome is an overview of how innovation measurement practices fit with more general performance measurement practices in the company; how the company balances qualitative and quantitative measures of innovation; and how frequent, and in which areas, follow-up occurs on various activities that are driving innovation directly and indirectly. This approach to improving innovation measurement practices can be applied to all types of innovation (radical and incremental, service and technology, etc.).

Companies should also examine what innovation tools and methodologies are available and used, as well as existing routines for innovation measurement. These activities provide a thorough understanding of the baseline, or starting point, of a company's innovation measurement practices. This knowledge is necessary to ensure that companies don't change measurement practices based on faulty conclusions due to a lack of homework.

Step 2: Assess the current innovation focus and set priorities. Different types of innovation require different types of measurement. Therefore, companies trying to measure innovation must clarify their innovation focus and priorities. For example, radical innovation calls for a different measurement practice than more incremental forms of innovation. History is full of companies that developed a product that transformed the way business was done in a particular industry. However, the notion that innovation is solely about game-changing ideas, while dramatic, is misleading. Indeed, many companies have generated big returns from product line extensions and incremental innovations.

Once your strategic ambitions are set, it's time to set priorities. Not everything can be accomplished at once, and prioritizing is an important aspect of innovation measurement. Here, companies need to understand that not all measures help with prioritization. Many results-based measures—for instance, those related to sales, profits, or customer loyalty—are based on lagging indicators. Such measures may be good for evaluating

It's critical for companies to carefully work through, agree on, and articulate measures that help sustain a deliberate and explicit innovation focus with clear priorities.

long-term effects, but they do not necessarily provide meaning-ful, short-term guidance. Specifically, lagging indicators don't help executives prioritize which innovation activities they need to undertake, when, and in what order. Nor do they help determine which people to involve in a project, which issues need immediate attention, and which ones can wait.

It's critical for companies to carefully work through, agree on, and articulate measures that help sustain a deliberate and explicit innovation focus with clear priorities. If not, they risk falling into both the first trap (measuring too much or too little) and the second (paying attention to the parts but missing the whole). A final point involves the importance of combining qualitative and quantitative measures. Many of the companies in our study relied on quantitative measures. However, some companies also used qualitative measures and found them to be an important complement to the quantitative measures in clarifying innovation focus and priorities.

Phase B: Improve Core Innovation Measurement Practices

Once companies have mapped their current innovation measurement practices and clarified their innovation focus and priorities, they can move on to updating existing measures or creating new ones. The focus of this second phase is to identify and develop suitable measures of innovation. In doing so, three broad categories should be considered: measures of the *overall portfolio*, measures of the *innovation process*, and measures of individual *innovation projects*.[4] Together, these activities will help companies avoid the second trap we identified: measuring individual parts but not the whole.

In our research, many companies struggled with combining these different dimensions. One reason was that different stakeholders have different innovation foci. If the development of innovation measures fails to balance the interests of different internal groups, there is a clear risk (as indicated by the third trap) that the company will end up with a fragmented and inconsistent measurement system. This is not to say that purposeful and agreed-upon innovation measures are completely free from tensions and conflicts. As in all operations, there are trade-offs between different goals such as speed, resource utilization, and risk taking; these trade-offs become painfully explicit when designing performance measures for the innovation portfolio, processes, and projects. But whichever measures a company selects need to advance the innovation strategy, with each measure providing clear answers to the questions of what is being measured, for whom, and why. This will help the company evaluate the usefulness of the measure and, later on, the assessment of goal achievement.

Important questions to answer in Phase B include:

- Do you have a balanced set of measures for your innovation portfolio, processes, and projects?
- Do you have the right number of measures?
- To what extent are the measures aligned with your strategy?
- To what extent do the measures contain potential conflicts?

Step 3: Develop or improve measures for evaluating the innovation portfolio. Companies increasingly apply portfolio thinking to their innovation priorities, seeking to balance radical innovation with incremental innovation, large projects with small projects, and high-risk innovation with low-risk innovation.[5] In essence, portfolio thinking involves assessing innovation efforts as a group rather than individually. To accomplish this, existing measures may need to be adapted.

The global consumer goods company we studied provides a good example of how portfolio thinking works. Management developed a matrix to illustrate the difference between breakthrough projects, projects to create the next generation of an existing product, and cost-saving projects. The vertical axis reflected the technological or business-model change required (whether the project involved no change, evolutionary new changes, or radical new changes) while the horizontal axis represented customer perception of the degree of novelty in use. Overall, the matrix had 12 categories. The matrix enabled management to evaluate projects and assess whether the overall mix was in line with the company's focus and priorities.

This company's practice underscores the importance of thinking carefully about the portfolio balance. By working through and agreeing on the desired composition of the innovation portfolio, companies can clarify which projects are apt to be short-term wins and which ones are long term and less certain. Doing so makes the link between innovation measurement and innovation strategy explicit.

Step 4: Develop or improve measures for evaluating the innovation process. Research on best practices for new product development has found that most companies have well-functioning processes for their innovation efforts. A formally documented new product development process has been the norm for many years.[6,7] The models often feature five to seven overlapping stages, separated by predefined decision points for evaluating progress. These decision points have various deliverables and criteria to help managers make go or no-go decisions.

Where companies often run into problems, as we saw with the companies we surveyed, is with identifying a balance of measures for the innovation process. Some companies emphasized measuring the number of ideas generated or the size of the R&D budget, resulting in a fight for resources and attention later on as projects evolved and some stalled. Other companies focused too much on outputs and did not consider how long it took to go from an idea to a product in the marketplace.

In our view, companies should treat inputs, throughputs, and outputs with equal emphasis when developing or improving measures for evaluating the innovation process. Companies can go beyond measuring only the number of projects launched and also measure the speed in the innovation process (for example, performance against schedule, duration of the process, or average time to market). Additionally, when innovation projects stall, it is possible to monitor the amount of time a project has been static and the reasons for the lack of progress. Finally, companies do need to measure outputs (such as new product sales as a percentage of total sales, or profits from new product sales).

Step 5: Develop or improve measures for evaluating innovation projects. Most innovation activities are conducted through projects. In addition to developing innovation measures for the company's portfolio and innovation processes in the aggregate, management needs to ensure that measurement also addresses the type and quantity of resources assigned to different innovation projects. In our study, two types of project measures emerged as particularly important. The first was the measurement of "slack" (the pool of resources available for producing a given level of organizational output).[8] We found that better-performing companies ran fewer innovation projects but spent more time on each one, ultimately achieving successful projects at a lower cost.[9] When there's slack, key individuals for a project are less likely to be bottlenecks.[10] Although many companies treat innovation projects as if they are predictable, innovation projects are in fact intrinsically uncertain and often include periods of slow progress due to lack of access to key individuals or resources.[11] The ability to measure slack can counterbalance this uncertainty and lead to better innovation management.

The second type of measure was related to customer feedback and experimentation. This includes when and how often an innovation project interacts with customers and seeks their feedback on products, or when it might make sense to develop prototypes.

Phase C: Deploy the Improved Innovation Measurement Practices

In this final phase, companies need to implement and reinforce their chosen innovation measures to ensure they are actually being used, while discarding old measures that are no longer needed. Once companies reach this phase, they cannot afford to sit back and relax. As a rule, companies should be prepared to review and revise their innovation measurement practices regularly.

Step 6: Set routines for innovation measurement. A key activity is to set realistic targets for each of the measures identified in the prior phase. To enhance the likelihood of meeting the targets and obtaining internal commitment, management needs to designate owners for each measure.[12] When setting targets, it's also important to think specifically about measurement frequency (for example, whether it should be weekly, monthly, quarterly, or annually).

Step 7: Implement the new innovation measures and routines. Once targets are established, companies should provide training and follow up to make sure that people are properly using the new innovation measures. Managers need to determine specifically how to roll out the measures efficiently and to whom they should apply.

Finally, managers should develop a process for reevaluating the innovation measures and for examining the cause-and-effect relationships between measures and results. In addition to full-scale annual reviews, managers may want to make interim adjustments on a quarterly or semiannual basis to ensure that the measures are working as intended.[13] In any case, executives should ask themselves how often and under what circumstances they will review their innovation measurement practices.

Why the Measurement Process Matters

In their efforts to become more innovative, companies are increasingly analyzing their innovation strategies, activities, processes, and projects. Evaluating and measuring innovation is central to these efforts. Although academics studying innovation measures previously downplayed the process through which measurement happens, we believe that approach has hindered the establishment of effective and efficient innovation measurement practices. Our framework is designed to help both individual executives and companies take control of their innovation measurement and understand the critical decisions, traps, and trade-offs involved—thereby allowing organizations to realize the full benefit of their innovation measurement efforts.

Notes

1. R. Adams, J. Bessant, and R. Phelps, "Innovation Management Measurement: A Review," *International Journal of Management Reviews* 8, no. 1 (2006): 21–47; S. D. Anthony, M. W. Johnson, and J. V. Sinfield, "Institutionalizing Innovation," *MIT Sloan Management Review* 49, no. 2 (2008): 45–53; European Committee for Standardization, "Innovation Management—Part 1: Innovation Management System," CEN/TS 16555–1 (Brussels, Belgium: CEN, 2013); OECD, *Oslo Manual: Guidelines for Collecting and Interpreting Innovation Data*, 3rd edition (Paris, France: OECD Publishing, 2005); A. R. Shapiro, "Measuring Innovation: Beyond Revenue from New Products," *Research-Technology Management* 49, no. 6 (2006): 42–51; and E. Mankin, "Measuring Innovation Performance," *Research-Technology Management* 50, no. 6 (2007): 5–7.

2. J. Platt, "Social Traps," *American Psychologist* 28, no. 8 (1973): 641–651.

3. R. M. Kanter, "Innovation: The Classic Traps," *Harvard Business Review* 84, no. 11 (2006): 72–83; and L. Välikangas and M. Gibbert, "Boundary-Setting Strategies for Escaping Innovation Traps," *MIT Sloan Management Review* 46, no. 3 (2005): 58–65.

4. European Committee for Standardization, "Innovation Management—Part 1"; OECD, *Oslo Manual*; Shapiro, "Measuring Innovation"; and Mankin, "Measuring Innovation Performance."

5. S. K. Markham and H. Lee, "Product Development and Management Association's 2012 Comparative Performance Assessment Study," *Journal of Product Innovation Management* 30, no. 3 (2013): 408–429; and R. G. Cooper, S. J. Edgett, and E. J. Kleinschmidt, "Benchmarking Best NPD Practices II," *Research-Technology Management* 47, no. 3 (2004): 50–59.

6. G. Barczak, A. Griffin, and K. B. Kahn, "Perspective: Trends and Drivers of Success in NPD Practices: Results of the 2003 PDMA Best Practices Study," *Journal of Product Innovation Management* 26, no. 1 (2009): 3–23.

7. Cooper, Edgett, and Kleinschmidt, "Benchmarking Best NPD Practices II"; and R. G. Cooper, "What's Next?: After Stage-Gate," *Research-Technology Management* 57, no. 1 (2014): 20–31.

8. N. Nohria and R. Gulati, "Is Slack Good or Bad for Innovation?" *Academy of Management Journal* 39, no. 5 (1996): 1245–1264.

9. Markham and Lee, "Product Development and Management Association's 2012 Comparative Performance Assessment Study."

10. A. Richtnér, P. Åhlström, and K. Goffin, "'Squeezing R&D': A Study of Organizational Slack and Knowledge Creation in NPD, Using the SECI Model," *Journal of Product Innovation Management* 31, no. 6 (2014): 1268–1290.

11. A. De Meyer, C. H. Loch, and M. T. Pich, "Managing Project Uncertainty: From Variation to Chaos," *MIT Sloan Management Review* 43, no. 2 (2002): 60–67; D. Reinertsen and L. Shaeffer, "Making R&D Lean," *Research-Technology Management* 48, no. 4 (2005): 51–57; N. Modig and P. Åhlström, *This Is Lean: Resolving the Efficiency Paradox* (Halmstad, Sweden: Rheologica Publishing, 2012).

12. A. Papalexandris, G. Ioannou, G. Prastacos, and K. E. Soderquist, "An Integrated Methodology for Putting the Balanced Scorecard into Action," *European Management Journal* 23, no. 2 (2005): 214–227.

13. Markham and Lee, "Product Development and Management Association's 2012 Comparative Performance Assessment Study."

IV

The People Part

13

When Innovation Meets the Language of the Corner Office

Dave Rochlin

At the University of California, Berkeley, our Haas@Work program regularly works with corporate partners on innovation challenges, design literacy, and the tools and processes that support vibrant innovation functions inside large companies.

We have learned that innovation executives often feel poorly understood by their fellow executives. In turn, functional executives are often baffled by what they see and hear from their innovation teams.

This isn't a big surprise. As with other business disciplines, innovation experts have their own language. Innovation processes now include *journey mapping, need finding, technology scouting, business model canvasing, prototyping, design sprints,* and more. While these processes and terms are becoming more widely used across organizations, they are not always fully embraced at the executive level.

At the same time, executives have their own unique language and tools, often derived from the strategy consulting firms embedded on the "executive floor" of organizations.

Effective innovation emphasizes divergent thinking to generate a variety of options in a relatively open-ended and unstructured way before determining the ultimate opportunity to pursue. Innovation executives will refer to this methodology as "bottom up," "exploratory," or "customer centered." The innovation journey is sometimes represented visually in an even less structured way, as part of a "fuzzy front end" of learning, experimentation, and exploration.

In contrast, strategy firms frequently use a highly structured approach to identify mutually exclusive and completely exhaustive—"MECE"—options, often based on a senior leader's hypothesis. This is called "top down," "hypotheses driven," or "answer first."

We recently held a workshop to explore the power—and constraints—of language and processes. Attending were San Francisco Bay area innovation executives, the consulting company McKinsey & Co., and McKinsey's design partner LUNAR. The goal was to look at how the languages and process of innovation and strategy consulting differ, and what the implications were for innovation leaders in communicating their work and making "asks" at the executive level.

We split the group in half and gave each team a case on digital transformation in the music industry, focused on the implications of the rise of streaming and subscription models. The case was the same, but one group (the innovation team) was guided to approach the problem from an exploratory method (for example, insights → problem frame → idea generation → proposed concept), while the other group examined it through a strategy lens (hypothesis development → issue tree → recommendation). We then had the groups present to each other and discuss the two different approaches.

As we expected, the strategy team's presentation focused on the key strategic issue of raising average revenue per user in digital models, and outlining how current models could be altered to achieve it.

The Contrast in Methodology between Innovationists and Strategists

The innovationist   The innovation journey   The strategist

The innovation team's presentation differed significantly. It focused first on examining consumer habits and preferences, and then on using the insights to propose new offerings that consumers would likely respond to.

Other observations from the experiment:

Strategists thought, "We were the boring team." Several of the innovation executives assigned to the strategy team felt constrained: Presenting in a structured, top-down approach left little room for conveying the excitement of the opportunity. For innovationists, the work of finding and conveying the "right problem" is a journey that is often the key to developing the ultimate solution. Presenting like a strategist, they said, felt like reading only the CliffsNotes version of a novel.

Innovationists commented, "Oh crap, why didn't we talk about that?" On the flip side, the innovation team initially felt much more comfortable presenting, but after observing the strategy team, they immediately recognized the value of a top-down, structured argument in swaying executive decision making. The strategy presentations pinpointed a governing idea much more quickly and succinctly, which was more likely to convince executives to take action.

It's the innovators' job to translate the conversation. Communicating across languages almost always requires significant work. While meeting in the middle or encouraging CEOs to cross-train in the language of innovation is a noble thought, asking executives to switch mindsets is not likely to fit the cadence of their workday. This means that it is innovationists who need to become more bilingual and strategy fluent—able to present in the style that management consulting firms use when making formal recommendations, updates, or requests. No matter how the work is generated, the final read out should include concrete problem statements and recommendations up front, backed up by supporting arguments and data. Innovation bilingualism also means being sensitive to the large amount of other activity on a typical executive's plate: Between meetings, a CEO may not have had a chance to give an innovator's project any thought.

Presenting insights to date can be a useful tool. A thorny issue for innovationists is the "work-in-process problem." As one of our design hosts described it: "In the middle of a typical project, we're still playing with insights and ideas, but the strategy guys already want content for their slides identifying the answer." While the top-down strategy method always has a central, guiding hypothesis, the exploratory method starts with a wide variety of possible problem statements and even more solutions—most of which are discarded along the way. Providing an update on activities at a mid-point can therefore be particularly distressing for both sides. One solution that surfaced during our workshop: distill innovation work in progress into discrete, clearly valuable insights that more closely resemble updates shared by strategy firms. For example, identifying key consumer insights to date would be of greater impact to executives than describing the entire journey.

Is there room for storytelling in making a compelling case for a new direction? Absolutely. The language of customer need is one that everyone speaks. But the structure and language of the story should match the audience. When speaking to executives, innovation leaders should make sure they are not only heard, but understood.

14

Why Learning Is Central to Sustained Innovation

Michael Ballé, James Morgan,
and Durward K. Sobek II

We frequently visit companies where managers say they want
to improve their product development capability. They want to
learn how lean principles and practices can improve their ability
to innovate while reducing costs and improving quality. When
we inquire about their approach to human resource development, we often hear, as one vice president of product development recently told us, that "of course, people are our most
important asset. So, we recruit and hire the top people from the
best universities and get out of their way."

However, the only things many companies actually do under
the heading of people development is to have an annual train-
ing-hours target and a travel budget for sending employees to
conferences. If managers *really* thought that people were their
greatest asset, and that it's the energy and creativity of their
employees that drives innovation, why do companies do so little? Why doesn't growing and developing people excite them
just as much as installing new additive manufacturing equipment or the latest cloud-based collaboration tool?

In studying manufacturing over the past two decades, we
have learned that operational excellence is not achieved by just

Until organizations view people as central (and leaders act accordingly), the risk that development process improvement efforts will not improve anything is frighteningly high.

applying so-called "lean" practices to every process. More than anything, it requires cultivating an aptitude and an expectation for continuous improvement within every employee.[1] Similarly, we learned from studying lean product development that *people, not processes, make great products.*

We frequently encounter managers who think improvements in the development process will pay off in better products. But better products don't just appear out of thin air: They are created by developers working with better knowledge and supported by good design processes.

The final design, including the product, manufacturing, and supply chain specifications, is the product of a complex network of interrelated technical decisions. How developers interact in the decision-making process—everything from framing problems, choosing ideas, and negotiating constraints to testing prototypes—is what shapes the product. In more transactional systems such as manufacturing or accounting, good processes usually produce a good outcome. What's important in lean product development isn't just whether you follow the right steps but how the work is done. Indeed, there are plenty of cases where companies followed "good" processes but had terrible results. The natural response is for managers to blame the process and then to add more best practices, increase the number and rigor of checkpoints, and change their flowcharts. Yet more often than not, the results continue to fall short. Until organizations view people as central (and leaders act accordingly), the risk that development process improvement efforts will not improve anything is frighteningly high.

The term "lean product development" is relatively new, but the underlying concepts have been around for more than three decades.[2] In the 1980s, an MIT study found that Japanese automotive companies followed practices that were profoundly different from those of other auto manufacturers, from the factory floor to new product development to supply chain management. The researchers began referring to the efficiency of the Japanese approaches as "lean."[3] Subsequent research focused specifically on Toyota Motor Corp.'s development practices as compared with those of its North American competitors.[4] As companies have applied the research to other areas, knowledge about lean development has deepened.[5] However, the critical role of people seems to have been overlooked.

About the Research

This article draws on our collective research and experience in lean manufacturing and lean product development over the past two decades. Two of us (Morgan and Sobek) conducted our doctoral research on Toyota's product development system. This work codified many of the foundational ideas underpinning current models of lean product development. Morgan subsequently worked at Ford as a global engineering director, where he deepened his understanding of lean product development through an in-depth collaboration with Mazda and helped transform Ford's product development capability. Sobek continued to develop the concepts through experiments and observation in academic and industrial settings. Our third author (Ballé) did part of his doctoral research on Toyota's collaboration with a key supplier and improvement of both the manufacturing process and product design. He has studied organization transformation problems for years through a large number of "lean transformation" initiatives. The ideas presented in this article are intended to assimilate our collective knowledge from research and practice into a useful framework.

As John Shook, CEO of the Lean Enterprise Institute, explained it, "The most important accomplishment of [Toyota] is simply that it has *learned to learn*."[6] Rather than being a state, lean is really a process by which companies can simultaneously improve product design, manufacturing capability, and supply chain efficiency. In new product development, lean is about advancing developer skills through technical training and methods of collaboration so that each developer is able to design, develop, and deliver better products and services.[7] Lean product development hinges upon having developers achieve individual mastery as the essential building block for better products—not delegating the overall responsibility to the human resources department. Companies can promote *individual mastery* by repeatedly asking three fundamental questions: (1) What do we need to learn about our customers, products, and production processes to design better products? (2) How do we learn this? (3) And finally, what kinds of organizational structures and routines will best support learning?

Question 1: What do we need to learn about our customers, products, and production processes to design better products?

With lean product development, the development process is geared toward introducing a constant *stream* of products at a steady rhythm (or, in lean terms, "takt"), as opposed to executing separate projects. From this perspective, a product such as Apple Inc.'s iPhone is a *value stream* made up of iPhone 1, iPhone 2, and so on, released at a steady pace. The idea is to be a little bit faster than the industry's natural rhythm of innovation.

Thinking in terms of a stream of products has significant impacts on the design process. Most new products aren't designed from scratch but evolve within the value chain. In some cases, the initial product provides a way to test an idea, which can be refined based on the response.[8] Toyota's first Prius, for instance, wasn't designed to gain a large share of the auto market. Engineers were actually surprised by the car's commercial success after it became popular in Hollywood. The aim of the first Prius was to prove that hybrid engines made sense. With the second Prius, Toyota wanted to make the technology acceptable to mainstream users. Now there is a stream of Prius models with significant market share, with hybrid technology being used in other car segments, including sport utility vehicles and minivans.

In an existing value stream of products, some product features will change, but many will not. The development challenge within a value stream, then, is not about creating the killer product that will overtake the market but improving the value proposition of existing solutions so that current customers are motivated to upgrade and potential customers are compelled to buy the product for the first time. Increasing the value involves learning about three main aspects of the product design upfront: (1) *fit to market*—how to reduce annoying features and offer new ones that fit today's customers' preferences; (2) *fit to manufacturing*—how to design a product that is less costly to build with better quality; and (3) *fit to industry*—how to exploit the opportunities in the supply chain to get more from the network of suppliers and the technical advances they offer.

A good place to start is fixing problems with the existing product. Just as a company doing lean manufacturing will attempt to solve quality issues in the current product, development teams applying lean fix whatever quality issues exist now and make improvements for future products. Take, for example, a company that manufactures gasoline dispensers, which succeeded in doubling unit sales over just a few years. Previously, engineers accepted recurrent customer complaints about rust on metal panels as a fact of life when machines are exposed to moisture. But they decided to tackle each issue one by one, improving product quality. Then they focused on the product's central functions and redesigned important components to improve the machine's performance and the value it offered customers (who consisted of both gas station owners and motorists). The process led to a popular new product that has helped sustain growth in sales and market share.

Building in quality in engineering means conducting a value analysis of how products can be improved and then figuring out which features customers would like in a new product. With lean product development, the idea is to look at products as evolving value streams and each product release as an opportunity to learn about where the market is going.

Question 2: How do we learn what we need to know? Just as important as what developers need to learn is *how* they learn. Improving each new product in the value stream depends on individual or team competence in being able to solve the immediate technical problems and to interface with what others are doing. Developers need to understand how their decisions impact manufacturing and the company's supply chain. This, of course, is a tall order, requiring both knowledge and rapid learning. The faster a development team is able to learn and the more knowledge the team has access to, the leaner (and more productive) the result.

The educational process in which people work and learn together by grappling with real issues is known as action learning.[9] Rather than acquiring knowledge through traditional methods, they learn on the job through a mentored process as the work is carried out.[10,11] In a lean product development framework, action learning revolves around using standards, solving problems creatively, and testing models against the physical world.

Standards

Lean differs from the typical development workflow in that it doesn't try to specify or "freeze" technical solutions up front. In fact, the goal is to postpone key decisions as much as possible to avoid hitting unforeseen barriers later on.[12] What lean does try to specify are the things that should be fixed and the things that should be flexible. By making these determinations early, engineers know where they have flexibility and where they must operate within fixed constraints. Deciding what's fixed and what's flexible isn't simply a feature of the development process—it's part of the training process for skilled engineers.

Tackling the fixed and the flexible require different approaches. Standards apply to the fixed elements. They are most powerful when they are based on experience with previous products, because the impact of specific decisions is known, and not following them may lead to problems. In their most elaborate form, standards inform developers about the known performance limits and trade-offs.[13] Lean developers use a variety of standards, including design standards that relate parameter values to performance, manufacturing standards that define current manufacturing capability, and development process standards that establish quality or test criteria.

Standards help developers make good decisions quickly because learning passes from one project to the next; there is no need to invest time and resources to learn the same things again. At the same time, new team members quickly acquire experiential knowledge by learning and applying it to their first projects, while experienced developers use standards to scaffold their own learning and transfer that learning to others.

Creative Problem Solving

Areas identified as flexible or to which current standards do not apply require creative problem solving. However, rather than responding to the first thought that comes to mind and then improving on it through iteration, it's important to explore many different options at once and to pursue them until it's clear, through aggressive testing and cross-functional evaluation, that they aren't feasible. The aim is to fully understand the design space underlying the problem in order to find a solution that works before committing to it.[14] Ideally, this "set-based" process will not only lead to a viable solution but also result in a preliminary set of standards that can be applied to the next project.

Whereas applying standards is a convergent thinking process intended to solve a problem rapidly by reusing existing knowledge, set-based concurrent engineering is a divergent thinking process that encourages developers to generate differing theories about a specific situation and test them until they are disproved or a clear winner emerges. Both thinking processes are essential for creativity, but they can be misapplied if fixed and flexible are confused. Developers need to know how to move seamlessly between the two modes, and leaders must recognize when to force the appropriate mode of thinking.

To illustrate, we learned at Toyota's technical center in Japan that manufacturing process standards were fed into the development process at the earliest stages, and in most situations the product design was forced to conform to the standards.[15] In essence, the process was predesigned, and the product design followed. It went beyond simply using the same processes and sequences across several products; based on experience, Toyota process engineers identified the key elements required to set a world-class standard for manufacturing excellence in all of their manufacturing processes (for example, limits on machinability of specific materials and geometries, or locations of grab points for material handling, part location, etc.), and they developed standards based on that knowledge. As new products were designed, the same processes and equipment could be used as long as the product designs complied with the standards. From the early stages in the process, the process engineers knew that the product design either *could* or *could not* be produced. In special cases where the need for expanded manufacturing capability arose, Toyota assigned a high-powered team to coinnovate new products and new processes as one integrated system.

Testing Models

The nature of development work requires developers to use models as representations of what they hope to build—anything from sketches and hypotheses to 3-D models and computer simulations. Most engineers recognize that engineering problems get solved through a mixture of going back to first principles and tinkering with concrete solutions. However, lean thinking has taught us that the quality of the models contributes enormously to both the quality and the speed of the solutions. Simulating solutions and testing them against existing standards, whether digitally, through analytical modeling, or even by trying things out with cardboard and tape, is central to learning for developers.

Models are incredibly important tools, because they are the medium of expression of new ideas and the means of assessing the suitability of ideas without creating the actual thing—making it feasible to look at many more ideas and to learn about them quickly and efficiently. However, models can't represent reality exactly. Indeed, problems can arise when decisions are made with an overreliance on models. As a result, the need to discover how well models predict the physical world leads to several practices that have come to characterize truly "lean" product development. For example:

- A design may seem great on paper, but a detailed review by one or more experienced designers can identify potential weaknesses. Design reviews provide an excellent opportunity to make the actual progress of development visible and to train younger developers. When conducted with cross-functional partners, such reviews can lead to tremendous learning at the intersections of disciplinary boundaries.

- Computer simulations may predict the behavior of a design concept, but only by observing a design in its intended context (what's known as the "gemba" in lean terminology) can we verify that the computer model has accounted for all of the significant variables.

- Building a prototype may be the best way to get a preliminary glimpse at how the item can be built. Developers relying solely on mental or virtual visualizations often overlook critical details that can make a huge difference in manufacturability.

- Physical testing should be done early and often to determine how well the concept meets requirements and to understand the design trade-offs.[16] Rather than testing merely to see if the design meets specifications or requirements, development teams should attempt to learn as much as possible from tests about how a design performs over a range of parameter values and its performance limits.

Question 3: What organizational structures and routines will support the learning? Given that the ability to develop successful new products depends on learning, what structures do managers need to establish to extend the reach of learning? One important structure is the development process itself. From a lean development perspective, the best processes encourage learning and teamwork rather than demanding adherence to a rigorously detailed workflow. With that in mind, an effective lean development process consists of five overlapping phases:[17]

- **Phase 1:** An early concept phase in which the project owner or core team defines the value proposition and where the fixed/flexible aspects of the product are fleshed out.
- **Phase 2:** A preliminary design, or study, phase where the main flexible domains are explored for alternative solutions and functional departments seek agreement in how to realize the desired concept at the subsystem level.
- **Phase 3:** A detailed design phase that is based on applying standards.
- **Phase 4:** A preproduction phase for ironing out how to organize the manufacturing system and supply chain to produce the new product.
- **Phase 5:** A tooling and prototype phase that involves interacting with suppliers.

The different phases reflect the inherently creative nature of product development. Because they depend on learning—that is, what's needed next depends on what's being learned in the current activity—highly detailed project planning is difficult. Phase 1, for example, includes both customer "immersion" to assess customer needs and technological immersion to understand the limits and capabilities of existing solutions. Based on this learning, developers can create product concepts or draft product brochures to share with expert groups. Then, based on discussions, the team will make decisions about which aspects of the concept will conform to the standard (which may require changes to the initial concept) and which areas are flexible (where products may need to go beyond existing standards, requiring innovation). Phase 1 concludes with a sharply defined product concept, timeline, and resource plan that all cross-functional partners agree to support. At Toyota, concept approval is a board-level event.

Phase 2, which is essentially a study phase, focuses on aspects of the product that are viewed as flexible. The idea is to consider several alternatives for each subsystem, to test and weed out the weak ideas, and to ensure compatibility with interfacing subsystems and with manufacturing capability before committing to a given solution. The process continues until the design converges on a solution that works from every relevant perspective. For example, a new car concept might be based on significant amounts of weight reduction while simultaneously having high levels of torsional stiffness (for better handling) and new standards for pedestrian protection. Manufacturing engineering and the designers of interfacing parts for capability with existing systems would review the various options. The alternatives that best meet the system of standards and constraints would be selected for further refinement.

Making the study phase lean requires pursuing the minimum information needed to kill an idea and holding off on detailed design and product simulation until the last possible moment. Developing detailed designs too quickly (only to abandon the idea later) is wasteful if the necessary information could just as easily be obtained from a quick sketch or mock-up. Lean development teams eliminate risk by having a backup solution ready to go if the new ideas do not pan out. The study phase goes beyond simply determining whether a concept meets requirements to understanding the design limits and the nature of trade-offs. Having a deep understanding enables the team to make good decisions and limits the number of iterations required in later phases. Phase 2 concludes with a realistic architectural plan for each subsystem and major component, along with preliminary standards for novel designs that will be adopted.

If Phases 1 and 2 are appropriately resourced, the subsequent phases should run reasonably smoothly and not require the level of rework that often plagues conventional development processes.[18] Since teams rely heavily on standards to ensure robust designs, they can eliminate much of the unknown, which allows for effective application of detailed project planning tools and precise coordination of work between development subteams. Without the upfront work in Phases 1 and 2, there is too much uncertainty in Phases 3–5, which makes detailed project planning extremely difficult.

In addition to the development process, organizational structures should also support the learning processes of developers.[19] The chief engineer is responsible for the market success of the product and has the final sign-off on technical decisions. He or she is the product architect and makes the judgment calls on what should be included in the product and what should be left out. The chief engineer has no formal authority over design engineers but is the person who pulls the new product through the entire company, from design to manufacturing and supply chain.

The rest of the development organization is organized into teams within core areas of responsibility. The primary role of these functional groups is not to "manage" the developers but to act as on-the-job learning centers where senior practitioners pass on both the theory and the traditions of the job to less-experienced people in the form of knowledge standards and ways of practice. Product design is therefore a melding between the chief engineer's driving vision and the knowledge constraints of each development area. The various reviews that dot the development process are used as cross-functional learning events intended to make sure that engineering, marketing, manufacturing, and purchasing are on the same page about the fixed/flexible boundaries within a project.

Larger organizations can afford to have a group of chief engineers or a project management office and separate functional groups as departments or divisions. However, this may not be feasible for smaller organizations, where individuals need to wear several hats at once. However, the important thing is that someone acts in the chief engineer role—in other words, is responsible for vision, system architecture, and making sure that decisions are consistent with customer needs—and that individuals (or groups) maintain and apply knowledge standards in core areas.

Implications for Managers

If you are a manager responsible for developing new products or services, you can take several steps to advance the development of your people.

First, you can make technical mastery an expectation of your organization and build it into the reward system and into the way you work every day. Toyota has made developing "towering technical competence" central in grooming new engineers and made mentoring fundamental to engineering leadership requirements.[20] Ford Motor Co. did this by creating a technical maturity model for each functional area within body and stamping engineering and supported it in the way the company made job assignments, ran design reviews, and rewarded its engineers. Individuals were assessed on their technical capabilities according to the model, and then plans were made to increase the individual's technical maturity and were incorporated into the individual's performance evaluation. This created a strong incentive to pursue technical mastery—and encouraged people to stay within their functional areas longer in order to build deeper expertise, for which they were rewarded.

Second, you should develop design standards and use them. You can start with the knowledge that already resides within the organization—spend a couple of hours in front of a smart board with your experienced developers and ask them to lay out how they would design a particular subsystem or how they would advise a novice designer. After codifying that information into a user-friendly format, use the design guide as the starting point of the next development project. Once you have design standards, you need to systematically update them based on the learning gained on each development project. Toyota and other companies set aside one to two weeks of the development project timeline to pause and reflect on what they have learned on the current project that should be incorporated into their design standards, and then they do the additional development work to codify that learning into a reusable format. You will need to make explicit who owns which design standards. Ideally, it will be the same group of people who will be using them, to ensure that they are easy to use and relevant.

Third, you should hold regular (for example, weekly) technical design reviews with the explicit aim of growing people through action learning and cross-functional collaboration. Some of the key questions to ask (repeatedly, even *ad nauseam*) are: (1) What is the design standard for the particular device or test? (2) How does the current design compare to standard? and (3) Where are the data to prove it? As much as possible, hold the design reviews on location (for instance, in the test lab, prototype shop, or factory) rather than in a conference room, and with actual artifacts, so that people can touch, handle, and point to what they agree with or not.

Fourth, you should take a critical look at your organization's formal development process and ask the following questions:

- Who is responsible for deeply understanding the customer, creating the system architecture, and coordinating efforts to ensure that all decisions align with customer interests?

- What problems do you intend to solve for the customer, and what additional value should the company offer?

- To what extent are people able to identify early the fixed aspects of the design (where we're not going to deviate from standard) versus the flexible aspects? Are you having candid enough conversations with the development team about what is straightforward versus what is tricky or even impossible?

- Are you investing enough resources in the study phase to investigate the flexible areas? Does that phase conclude with enough clarity and certainty about the remaining challenges of the project?

- To what extent do process checkpoints encourage learning as opposed to meeting requirements or task lists? Do you have the right number of checkpoints, do they occur at the right points in time, and are the right people involved?

Finally, you should take stock of the leadership culture within the organization. To support learning, ask the leadership team to focus less on decision making and assigning work and more on instructing and improving. Design and manufacturing standards (what we currently know about the product and the technical processes) are the main tools for deepening the organization's understanding of products and production processes. Encouraging problem solving to resolve performance gaps with standards deepens the autonomy and insight of the responsible developers. Developer capacity is further enhanced by asking revealing questions about what people should be learning and how they are learning it.

Great people make great products. The explicit aim of lean product development is to grow better developers, who are increasingly knowledgeable and capable of solving problems and generating new solutions. People and people systems are the most important parts of a product development system, because people generate the knowledge necessary for innovation, and people apply that knowledge to designs for new products, new manufacturing systems, and more robust supply chains. Unfortunately, not every organization subscribes to this view—after all, it's easier to think in terms of process or tools solutions. However, both our research and our experience working with lean development organizations have helped us better understand what developers need to learn, how they learn it, and what organizational structures best support them. By applying these insights and making people the backbone of the development system, companies can achieve a triple win: increased innovation, faster time to market, and lower costs.

Notes

1. M. Ballé, G. Beauvallet, A. Smalley, and D. K. Sobek II, "The Thinking Production System," *Reflections* 7, no. 2 (2006): 1–12.

2. "Lean product development" is also referred to as "lean product and process development" to highlight the innovation involved both in new products and in the manufacturing systems needed to produce them. We use the shorter phrase in order to avoid confusion between manufacturing process and development process. Some similarities can also be found in the work on "lean startups," in which rapid learning techniques are applied to help entrepreneurs create new products or services with less waste and better chance for success.

3. J. P. Womack, D. T. Jones, and D. Roos, *The Machine That Changed the World* (New York: Rawson Associates, 1990).

4. See D. K. Sobek II, J. K. Liker, and A. Ward, "Another Look at Toyota's Integrated Product Development," *Harvard Business Review* 76, no. 4, (1998): 36–49; and J. M. Morgan and J. K. Liker, *The Toyota Product Development System: Integrating People, Process, and Technology* (New York: Productivity Press, 2006).

5. See, for example, A. C. Ward and D. K. Sobek II, *Lean Product and Process Development*, 2nd ed. (Cambridge, MA: Lean Enterprise Institute, 2014); R. Mascitelli, *Mastering Lean Product Development: A Practical, Event-Driven Process for Maximizing Speed, Profits, and Quality* (Northridge, CA: Technology Perspectives, 2011); D. G. Reinertsen, *The Principles of Product Development Flow* (Redondo Beach, CA: Celeritas Publishing, 2009); T. Schipper and M. Swets, *Innovative Lean Development* (New York: Productivity Press, 2010); and M. N. Kennedy, *Product Development for the Lean Enterprise* (Richmond, VA: Oaklea Press, 2003).

6. J. Shook, *Managing to Learn* (Cambridge, MA: Lean Enterprise Institute, 2008).

7. By "developer," we mean any person who plays a substantive role in the development of new products, including but not limited to marketers, product engineers, industrial designers, production engineers, prototypers, test engineers, and purchasers.

8. E. Ries, *The Lean Startup* (New York: Random House, 2011).

9. R. W. Revans, *Action Learning: New Techniques for Management* (London: Blond & Briggs, 1980).

10. S. Spear, "Learning to Lead at Toyota," *Harvard Business Review* 82, no 5 (2004): 78–86.

11. M. Ballé and P. Handlinger, "Learning Lean: Don't Implement Lean, Become Lean," *Reflections* 12, no. 1 (2012): 17–31.

12. A. Ward, J. K. Liker, J. J. Cristiano, and D. K. Sobek II, "The Second Toyota Paradox: How Delaying Decisions Can Make Better Cars Faster," *MIT Sloan Management Review* 36, no. 3 (1995): 43–61.

13. Ward and Sobek II, "Lean Product and Process Development."

14. B. M. Kennedy, D. K. Sobek II, and M. N. Kennedy, "Reducing Rework by Applying Set-Based Practices Early in the Systems Engineering Process," *Systems Engineering* 17, no. 3 (2014): 278–296.

15. Morgan and Liker, "The Toyota Product Development System."

16. For a thorough discussion of the power of experimentation, see S. Thomke, *Experimentation Matters* (Boston, MA: Harvard Business Press, 2003).

17. F. Ballé and M. Ballé, "Lean Development," *Business Strategy Review* 16, no. 3 (2005): 17–22.

18. S. Thomke and T. Fujimoto, "The Effect of 'Front-Loading' Problem-Solving on Product Development Performance," *Journal of Product Innovation Management* 17, no. 2 (2000): 128–142.

19. Ward and Sobek II, "Lean Product and Process Development."

20. Morgan and Liker, "The Toyota Product Development System."

15

Learning the Art of Business Improvisation

Edivandro Carlos Conforto, Eric Rebentisch, and Daniel Amaral

The ability to innovate and rapidly respond to changes in the business environment is critical to competitiveness and success. Creativity and problem-solving skills are key elements of improving the outcomes in projects that require innovation. Iterative development, improvisation, and experimentation combined with focus and flexibility are needed to identify new business opportunities and effectively execute projects. But business demands also require efficiency, and many organizations pursue disciplined project management and product development practices that emphasize standardization and consistency to help drive down costs.

Is a disciplined approach to product development at odds with creativity and improvisation? Can managers develop skills around building improvisation and creativity, especially for innovative projects? If so, what are the right conditions for improvisation to flourish? In this chapter, we discuss findings from our study on improvisation in product development projects and how managers can create a team environment conducive to improvisation.

Improvisation Fundamentals

In general terms, improvisation is the ability to create and implement a new or an unplanned solution in the face of an unexpected problem or change. It is often seen as a spontaneous, intuitive, creative problem-solving behavior that mostly happens "on the fly."

Improvisation has been studied for some time in the fields of music, psychology, and education. In the theater, it is often seen as a "pure" state of creativity, in which a team or individual may rely on intuition and spontaneity to come up with an action or arrangement. In music, researchers have identified different skills that when combined form the core competence for improvisation, including problem solving, communication and expression, proper use of language, creativity, and visualization abilities. Some have suggested that improvisation should itself be a discipline and be officially taught in music schools.

Improvisation has also been studied in organizational strategy and product development. Studies have found positive correlations between improvisation in product development and team performance. It is considered a spontaneous behavior (collectively or individually), and therefore dependent on team members' attitudes, experience, motivation, intuition, and individual skills. Despite a number of studies on improvisation in the management context, there is no consensus on the most effective approach to develop this competence in project teams.

As a part of an ongoing research program to understand the principles of agility and adaptability in project teams, we examined project and team characteristics related to improvisation practices in product development, software development, and the implementation of software projects. We surveyed project managers, program managers, portfolio managers, and project team members from 17 different industry sectors and 76 countries—856 professionals overall. One of our primary objectives was to understand the key factors associated with improvisation capabilities in project teams and their potential correlation with agility performance.

In the survey, we measured "improvisation practices" without explicitly mentioning or using the term "improvisation." We examined three different situations: (1) The project tasks were not assigned to the team members at a detailed level, but the team was provided with a macro vision of the project and had to figure out what tasks and activities had to be executed; (2) the project team applied an iterative learning execution approach to deal with unexpected changes and uncertainty during the project life cycle; and (3) the team combined new approaches (practices, tools, and techniques) to address different types of problems, changes, and opportunities during the project life cycle. In addition, we measured a number of team and organization characteristics that are related to agility performance.

We also asked respondents to self-declare the type of management approach (agile or traditional) that represented the majority of practices and tools applied to manage the project. The traditional or "waterfall" project management approach is mainly focused on long-term planning, requirements, stability, and well-defined and phase-oriented deliverables. Agile project management, by contrast, relies on iterative and incremental planning and execution processes in which requirements evolve and changes are quickly absorbed.

Improvisation in Innovation Projects

Innovation projects are inherently challenging to execute because of uncertainty and evolving opportunities to improve the ultimate solution. In general, these projects may have significant unknown requirements, volatile scope, and unidentified risks; the technology may be evolving continuously, and therefore the team may be unable to anticipate all tasks and outcomes. In order to succeed, the project team must be able to respond rapidly to changes, recognize opportunities to improve the product, and deliver results under time and cost pressures. They need to come up with solutions that may not have been planned or previously identified, adapt the project, plan accordingly, and get the work done.

We found that projects with extreme changes in requirements (90% or more changes) employed 41% more improvisation practices than projects that had relatively stable requirements (10% or fewer changes). This suggests that higher levels of improvisation, deliberate or not, are more likely to happen in projects that have fluid and unstable requirements. Furthermore, we observed that teams working on projects in which team members don't possess significant prior experience or technical knowledge were more likely to improvise than were experienced teams working on more familiar projects or technology. That effect appears to be consistent across different types of projects. For example, projects with greater levels of innovation (for example, a product or software totally new to the market) are more likely to result in greater levels of improvisation.

Overall, we observed that demands for more innovation, more changes in requirements, the degree of team experience in similar projects, and the degree of knowledge about the technology all were predictors of the level of improvisation displayed by the team. Each of these factors is a threat to project plans and could therefore trigger the need for improvisation by the team.

Improvisation might be simply a natural response to unexpected problems or new challenges. Or it might be part of a deliberate strategy for a team that understands that its product and project objectives will likely change during the course of the project. In either case, a team that is more skilled at improvisation will likely have a performance advantage in such a dynamic environment. Can the improvisation capabilities of the team be enhanced so that it is better able to more creatively adapt to unexpected changes in a project and turn a challenge into a source of competitive advantage? How might managers promote the right conditions to enable improvisation to occur when needed?

Creating Conditions That Foster Improvisation

Based on our research findings, we believe that the capacity of a team to improvise can be developed and enhanced. Focused effort in three areas can help develop these improvisation competencies.

Build a culture that recognizes and views changes positively. We found that greater levels of improvisation came from teams that displayed a positive attitude toward dealing with and accepting ambiguity and project changes. They also displayed a higher level of autonomy in making decisions.

In fast-paced and innovative project environments, teams should be empowered to make decisions locally, be informed about and willing to take risks, and not overly fear potential failure. This will help them to reduce uncertainty more quickly and effectively learn from their experiences. Teams equipped with a broad array of tools and techniques can use them to respond to different types of challenges. The focus should be on helping teams anticipate and recognize changing circumstances and make more rapid and accurate decisions.

Create the right team structure and project environment. Project teams with greater improvisation had more frequent meetings and interactions with project leaders and key stakeholders to discuss project-related issues. These meetings occurred at least once a week—and in some cases, every day. The meetings allowed more frequent face-to-face interactions focused on the project and improved communication quality. That, in turn, enabled teams to respond more quickly to changes.

We also saw greater levels of improvisation in smaller teams that displayed more self-directing and self-organizing characteristics, such as being responsible for monitoring and updating the status of their activities and deliverables. This allowed the project manager to stay focused on the aggregated information and on more strategic issues related to the project.

Provide management practices and tools that facilitate improvisation. Not surprisingly, teams with greater improvisation characteristics were more likely to use agile management approaches, techniques, and tools. In fact, teams that embraced an agile approach were nine times more likely to have high levels of improvisation compared with teams that used a more traditional (waterfall) approach.

The agile methods we observed in the teams with higher levels of improvisation included iterative development, supported by recurring delivery of higher-value deliverables; constant interactions between stakeholders and the project team; the use of visual tools to collaboratively manage the project with team members; and active involvement with the client and/or user in the development process.

Deliberately or not, project teams are improvising. Improvisation can foster problem solving, creativity, and innovation, and it is becoming a requirement for many organizations. Although improvisation might seem to be spontaneous and intuitive, to do it well requires the development of disciplined and deliberate processes and capabilities. Managers working in dynamic, fast-paced, and highly innovative project environments should develop and refine capabilities in these three areas to create a project environment that will enhance a team's improvisation competencies—ultimately with an eye toward improving project results and innovation.

Related Research

E. C. Conforto, E. Rebentisch, and D. Amaral, "The Building Blocks of Agility as a Team's Competence in Project Management" (Consortium for Engineering Program Excellence, Massachusetts Institute of Technology, Cambridge, MA, 2014).

E. C. Conforto, E. Rebentisch, and D. Amaral, "Developing Improvisation Capabilities to Help Project Teams Innovate" (working paper, Consortium for Engineering Program Excellence, Massachusetts Institute of Technology, Cambridge, MA, 2015).

Contributors

Daniel Amaral is a professor in the integrated engineering group at the University of São Paulo at São Carlos School of Engineering in São Carlos, Brazil.

Jamie Anderson is an adjunct professor of strategic management at the Antwerp Management School in Antwerp, Belgium.

Scott D. Anthony is the managing partner of Innosight, the growth strategy arm of Huron, a US-based diversified professional services firm. He is the lead author of *Dual Transformation: How to Reposition Today's Business While Creating the Future*. He has written six other books, including *Seeing What's Next* (with Harvard professor and Innosight cofounder Clayton M. Christensen), *The Little Black Book of Innovation*, and *The First Mile*.

Yun Mi Antorini is an assistant professor of business communication at Aarhus University in Aarhus, Denmark.

Michael Arena is chief talent officer at General Motors Co. in Detroit, Michigan.

Tormod Askildsen is senior director of community engagement and events at the Lego Group in Billund, Denmark.

Michael Ballé is an associate researcher at Télécom ParisTech's Project Lean Enterprise in Paris, France.

Thomas Bartman is a former senior researcher at the Forum for Growth and Innovation at Harvard Business School in Boston, Massachusetts.

Jennie Björk is a researcher at KTH Royal Institute of Technology in Stockholm, Sweden.

Marcel Bogers is an associate professor of innovation and entrepreneurship at the University of Copenhagen in Copenhagen, Denmark.

Anna Brattström is a postdoctoral fellow in the department of business administration at Lund University in Lund, Sweden.

Clayton M. Christensen is the Kim B. Clark Professor of Business Administration at Harvard Business School in Boston, Massachusetts.

Edivandro Carlos Conforto is a research affiliate at the Consortium for Engineering Program Excellence at the Massachusetts Institute of Technology in Cambridge, Massachusetts.

Rob Cross is the Edward A. Madden Professor of Global Business at Babson College in Babson Park, Massachusetts.

Charles Dhanaraj is a professor of strategy and global leadership at IMD in Lausanne, Switzerland.

Thomas Fink is the director of the London Institute for Mathematical Sciences as well as a researcher at France's National Center for Scientific Research in Paris, France.

Nicolai J. Foss is a professor of strategy and organization at Copenhagen Business School in Copenhagen, Denmark.

Johan Frishammar is a professor of entrepreneurship and innovation at Luleå University of Technology in Luleå, Sweden.

Johann Harnoss is a project leader in BCG's New York office and a core member of the company's corporate development, energy and strategy practices, as well as an ambassador to the BCG Henderson Institute.

Srivardhini K. Jha is a visiting professor of entrepreneurship at the Indian Institute of Management Bangalore in Bangalore, India.

Lâle Kesebi is the chief communications officer and head of strategic engagement at Li & Fung Ltd. in Hong Kong.

Rishikesha T. Krishnan is director and a professor of strategic management at the Indian Institute of Management Indore in Indore, India.

Martin Kupp is an associate professor of entrepreneurship and strategy at the Paris, France, campus of ESCP Europe.

Sean Looram is executive vice president at Li & Fung Ltd. in Hong Kong.

Mats Magnusson is a professor of product innovation engineering at KTH Royal Institute of Technology in Stockholm, Sweden.

Ann Majchrzak is the USC Associates Chair in Business Administration and a professor of data sciences and operations at the University of Southern California's Marshall School of Business in Los Angeles, California.

Arvind Malhotra is the H. Allen Andrew Professor of Entrepreneurial Education and professor of strategy and entrepreneurship at the University of North Carolina at Chapel Hill's Kenan-Flagler Business School in Chapel Hill, North Carolina.

James Morgan is a senior adviser to the Lean Enterprise Institute in Cambridge, Massachusetts.

Albert M. Muñiz Jr. is an associate professor of marketing at DePaul University in Chicago, Illinois.

Ramiro Palma is a project leader at the BCG office in Dallas, Texas, and a core member of the company's technology, media, and telecommunications practice.

Ishwardutt Parulkar is a distinguished engineer at Cisco Systems Inc. in Bangalore, India.

Eric Rebentisch is a research associate and directs the Consortium for Engineering Program Excellence at the Massachusetts Institute of Technology in Cambridge, Massachusetts.

Jörg Reckhenrich is an artist based in Berlin, Germany, as well as a faculty member of CEIBS Zurich Institute of Business Education in Zurich, Switzerland.

Martin Reeves is a senior partner and managing director in the BCG New York office and the director of the BCG Henderson Institute.

Anders Richtnér is an associate professor at the Stockholm School of Economics (SSE) as well as CEO of SSE Executive Education in Stockholm, Sweden.

Dave Rochlin is a lecturer in applied innovation at the Haas School of Business at the University of California, Berkeley, and executive director of the Haas@Work program.

Duncan Simester is the NTU Professor of Management Science and head of the marketing group at the Massachusetts Institute of Technology's Sloan School of Management in Cambridge, Massachusetts.

Jonathan Sims is an assistant professor of management at Babson College in Babson Park, Massachusetts.

Joseph V. Sinfield is an associate professor of civil engineering at Purdue University in West Lafayette, Indiana.

Durward K. Sobek II is a professor of mechanical and industrial engineering at Montana State University in Bozeman, Montana.

Freddy Solis is a postdoctoral research associate in the College of Engineering at Purdue University in West Lafayette, Indiana.

Kristian J. Sund is an associate professor of strategy and organization at Roskilde University in Roskilde, Denmark.

Mary Uhl-Bien is the BNSF Railway Endowed Professor of Leadership at the Neeley School of Business at Texas Christian University in Fort Worth, Texas.

Derek van Bever is a senior lecturer of business administration as well as director of the Forum for Growth and Innovation at Harvard Business School in Boston, Massachusetts.

J. Andrei Villarroel is a professor of innovation and entrepreneurship at the School of Management Fribourg in Fribourg, Switzerland.

Amy Webb is CEO of the Future Today Institute, which provides futures forecasting for business, government, and nonprofit clients, and the author of *The Signals Are Talking: Why Today's Fringe Is Tomorrow's Mainstream*.

Index